Sculpture Space

[the book]

For the artists and individuals who are
part of the Sculpture Space story

EDITED BY LIN SMITH VINCENT
WITH SYDNEY L. WALLER

Sculpture Space Inc., Utica, New York

[end leaf]

PETER BOWYER

Photograph by Sylvia de Swaan, 1983

[page 2]

TIM SCOFFIELD

Sculpture Space resident, 2001/2002

Photograph by Gina Murtagh

Sculpture Space [the book] is published on the occasion of the 30th anniversary of Sculpture Space Inc.; and is made possible with generous support from The Community Foundation of Herkimer & Oneida Counties, Inc., the Rosamond G. Childs Fund, Furthermore: a program of the J. M. Kaplan Fund and Brodock Press.

The Sculpture Space artists' workspace and residency program is supported by the New York State Council on the Arts, a public agency, and the National Endowment for the Arts, which believes that a great nation deserves great art. Additional support is provided by the Milton and Sally Avery Foundation, the Coleman Foundation, The Community Foundation of Herkimer & Oneida Counties, Inc., the Geraldine R. Dodge Foundation, the Pollock-Krasner Foundation, the Stephen F. Weaver Foundation and a growing circle of business sponsors and Friends. Its endowment fund is entrusted to The Community Foundation of Herkimer & Oneida Counties, Inc.

Sculpture Space is a founding member of the Alliance of Artist Communities, the National Association of Artists Organizations and the New York State Artists Workspace Consortium. The Consortium is supported by the New York State Council on the Arts, The Andy Warhol Foundation for the Visual Arts, the Ford Foundation and the National Endowment for the Arts.

Published by Sculpture Space Inc.
12 Gates Street
Utica, New York 13502
T 315-724-8381, F 315-797-6639
info@sculpturespace.org
www.sculpturespace.org

Design: DeNicola Design Inc., Cooperstown, New York
Printer: Brodock Press, Utica, New York
Cover image: Saya Woolfalk, *Winter Garden: Hybrid Love Objects* (detail), 2005; still from video by Bosung Kim

ISBN 9780979596902
Library of Congress Control number: 2007927757
First edition
Printed in Utica, New York, USA

State of the Arts

NYSCA

NATIONAL
ENDOWMENT
FOR THE ARTS

THE COMMUNITY FOUNDATION
OF HERKIMER & ONEIDA COUNTIES, INC.

Sculpture
Space
[the book]

Sculpture Space, Utica, New York; photograph by Gale Farley, 2007

To step into the Sculpture Space studio is to enter a remarkable crucible for the creative process. Artists work. Ideas take form. The invisible becomes visible. Alchemy happens: ordinary materials are transformed into the extraordinary. It's very exciting — and important. Unfettered artistic expression is a hallmark of civil society: to support its unlimited possibilities is a cultural imperative — and our mission.

Why sculpture? As Charlotta Kotik writes in these pages, sculpture is, by its very nature, provocative: it is multi-dimensional. Whether an installation, a video or sound environment, a performance or an object — or a combination thereof — it shares our space. It is also the art form we use as a nation and society to commemorate victories — and to memorialize tragedies. Artists in each generation contribute to the culture of their day. Artists at Sculpture Space contribute to the development of contemporary sculpture.

It is my honor and privilege to introduce *Sculpture Space [the book]*, a broad-brush overview of the story of that special place in the Mohawk Valley called Sculpture Space: how we began, who we are, what we do and why we do it and, especially, what we inspire: rich artistic creation in all its gritty glory. The history of Sculpture Space is a remarkable group effort, a saga of many stories. From the beginning the New York State Council on the Arts, chaired by the late Kitty Carlisle Hart, found merit in this undertaking. As with all Sculpture Space projects, and Sculpture Space itself, this publication represents a community of ideas. It is dedicated to all of the inventive, energetic, imaginative and hard-working individuals who have contributed to that community, seeing a new world of possibilities for Sculpture Space.

Anniversaries are occasions for reflection: moments to take stock and mark time. Our 30th anniversary has been the catalyst for this publication, and our program longevity a grand cause for celebration. We are humbled and pleased that so many esteemed colleagues beyond the studio agreed that this was so, among them Milton Bloch, president, and Paul Schweizer, director, of the Munson-Williams-Proctor Arts Institute, and David Nathans, acting director of Hamilton College's Emerson Gallery, who in 2003 independently explored possible anniversary exhibitions that they subsequently organized for their respective institutions.

Thanks to their vision and commitment, and that of their staffs and many other colleagues, the central New York community enjoyed a rich spectrum of celebratory activities — festive, scholarly, educational — over the two-year period, 2006/2007.

These events included a seven-site series of distinct exhibitions called *Sculpture Central International*; a symposium on public art at Hamilton College and Colgate University and a gala honoring the program's founders and leaders. They preceded this volume — which is something more permanent that we can hold onto when the shows are dismantled, the programs are over and the artists go home.

The 30th-anniversary steering committee, chaired by past board president Arlene Somer, formed an advisory publications committee that included Mary E. Murray, curator of modern and contemporary art at the MWPAI. The committee suggested themes and possible essayists. To the members we are grateful.

Distinguished authors responded with enthusiasm to the project: Thomas E. Piché, Jr., former senior curator at the Everson Museum in Syracuse and now director of the Gibson Gallery at SUNY Potsdam, skillfully highlights the history of the organization, the exceptional community of artists, staff and board volunteers who kept their sights on the vision and the concept a reality. New York City-based independent critic and curator Margaret Mathews-Berenson traveled to Utica in the winter of 2006 to observe the residency program firsthand; her research into the world of artists' residencies underscores what makes Sculpture Space unique. Renowned Brooklyn Museum curator and art historian Charlotta Kotik honors us with an intriguing overview of the state of contemporary sculpture, illustrating the explosion of genres and approaches to this most rambunctious of artistic disciplines. Art historian Rand Carter, longtime member of Utica's Landmarks Society and a professor at Hamilton College, offers an informative treatment of the architecture and history of our richly layered hometown.

We were extremely fortunate to retain the services of Lin Smith Vincent, past editor-in-chief of *Art and Auction* magazine, to edit and Doreen DeNicola and Brandy Toner of DeNicola Design Inc. to design our book. I am forever grateful for the privilege of working with these remarkable women, whose keen minds and consummate skills assured excellence across time zones and competing projects.

We were fortunate beyond measure that The Community Foundation of Herkimer & Oneida Counties, Inc., the Rosamond G. Childs Fund and Furthermore: a program of the J.M. Kaplan Fund found merit in the concept and awarded generous grants to make the publication a reality. We thank the staffs and boards of these organizations, especially Richard Hanna, then president of The Community Foundation, and Joan

Davidson, the visionary president of Furthermore. We owe a large debt of gratitude to our Utica neighbor Brodock Press for generously working with us.

I thank the many dedicated people who shared so much information about the early days at Sculpture Space. Charlie Fisher, Richard Friedberg and John von Bergen, the founding artist triumvirate, recalled many delicious memories of those first years, which coincided with what Michael Kimmelman calls the "scrappy 1970s, when art wasn't worth much [and] nothing was impossible." I also thank my predecessors, Sylvia de Swaan and Gina Murtagh, as well as our studio manager of 20 years, Jonathan Kirk, for their invaluable assistance. Sculpture Space thrives today in large part because of their dedicated stewardship.

A project of this magnitude would not be possible without the support of wonderful friends. I particularly wish to acknowledge Patterson Sims and Katy Homans for their counsel and support at strategic times during the project. I also thank Jason McCoy of Jason McCoy Inc. for generously hosting a book party in New York. I especially wish to acknowledge Colleen Kahler for her support in the office; consultant Elizabeth Schoonmaker, curatorial project manager for the 30th anniversary projects; and the Sculpture Space studio managers, Takashi Soga and Patrick Cuffe.

Additionally, I thank our hardworking board of directors for their encouragement and support as we undertook this project, one that is far beyond the ordinary sphere of support for artists. Recognizing its value, they made it possible for us to proceed. Thanks, too, to our former board members, the local artists, our state legislators, the city of Utica and the remarkable businesses and community volunteers who have helped us keep the doors open for 30 years and, we hope, on into the next century.

Finally, I thank the artists for their work: the current artists; the future artists who will come to make new work in this old factory building; and especially, the 400 alumni artists whose workstays at Sculpture Space define us. Like the factory workers who toiled in our space in years gone by, these artists work with their hands, and they work hard, with a wide range of tools. Their works were, and still are, forever in progress. And when they leave here, they take their creations with them out into the world — strong works of art, contemporary art, the art of our time.

Utica, New York | May 2007

9

Sculpture Space sits well back from the street, a one-story, clean-lined rectangular building framed by trees and surrounded by an open lot. Until December 2006, when a bright orange steel sign with six-foot lettering was installed on the roof, the prospect from nearby Whitesboro Street gave little indication of the activity that takes place inside the structure.[1] Indeed, a visitor might still miss the discrete sign that introduces the property at curbside, and the several large-scale sculptures scattered about the yard only hint at the life unfolding within the cement-block walls beyond.

Photographs dating from the mid-1970s reveal that the edifice that houses Sculpture Space was once part of a campus of brick and stone manufacturing buildings, some dating back to the mid-19th century, that made up the Utica Steam Engine & Boiler Works. The Boiler Works, then in operation since 1831 under various names, was a custom metal shop with specialized equipment and facilities designed to hoist, weld, cut, pierce and bend heavy metal into forms useful to industry.

Sculpture Space is today quartered in the one structure that remains from the Boiler Works operation, but that building bears little outer resemblance to its former industrial self. Once called the Federal Building, it was built as part of the works during the Second World War and outfitted with equipment appropriate for the construction of landing craft.[2] A gabled wooden portico that originally faced the structure has been removed, irregular building features have been unified, the lot cleared of refuse, and Sculpture Space now stands as a spare modern box. Its markedly uninflected exterior includes a narrow entrance surmounted by a glass-brick transom and, next to that, a large overhead door of commercial proportions. A long side wall, punctuated by several glass-brick windows, meets the approach of the gravely drive that leads to the building's entry.

Once inside, a visitor is met by an obviously purposeful workspace — 5,000 square feet of it — with a 15-foot-high ceiling. The expansive, open room is coolly lit by a series of ceiling-hung fluorescent lights and the daylight that filters through the glass-brick windows. Heavy-duty metal worktables, temporary walls and various pieces of bulky machinery, including table saws, presses, MIG and TIG welders, a plasma cutter, welding tanks (OXY-Acetylene, Argon, CO_2) and hoists, are stationed throughout. A freestanding steel stove, centrally placed, gives off a welcome heat that helps lower the interior chill held in place by the porous cement floor. Near the front door a steel-framed placard proclaims a statement of mission and faith. It reads, in part: "Sculpture Space is a laboratory of experimentation and creativity ... dedicated

SCULPTURE SPACE STUDIO
Photograph by Gale Farley, 2007

[page 10/11]

UTICA STEAM ENGINE & BOILER WORKS
Photograph by Sylvia de Swaan, c. 1980

[opposite]

JONATHAN KIRK
Work-in-progress at Sculpture Space
Photograph (detail) by Sylvia de Swaan, n.d.

to the needs of artists whose focus is sculpture." Since 1976, and with only slight refinements, this has been the admirable and continuous goal of this project.

The distance presented by the ensuing 30 years requires us to view the storied foundations of Sculpture Space through a scrim that is colored by black-and-white photographs, yellowing newspaper accounts, and the amber memories of those who were present. A certain history coalesces around the ideas that are generally held to be true: that in 1972 Charlie Fisher, son of one of the owners of the Utica Steam Engine & Boiler Works, returned home to Utica from college and began to study sculpture at the Munson-Williams-Proctor Institute School of Art; that in early 1974 Fisher suggested that his teacher, John von Bergen, make use of the machinery at the Boiler Works[3] to facilitate the construction of a large steel sculpture von Bergen had undertaken; and that by early 1975 von Bergen, pleased with the outcome of his encounter there, had arranged to set up a workspace in a corner of the by-now-fallow Federal Building at the Boiler Works. He looks back at this situation with pleasure: "I'd worked in lofts and even chicken coops, so this odd space didn't faze me. In fact, I was really excited by what I'd found. It's rare to locate a large enough space, much less one with access to machines and materials."[4]

During this same time period, another scenario was playing out in nearby Clinton, NY. Bernadine Lohden, director of the Kirkland Art Center, was host to Richard Friedberg, a Manhattan-based sculptor, who had received state funding to be artist-in-residence at the center during the summer of 1974 and, again, during the following spring. Lohden remembers it was not long before Friedberg and von Bergen would meet and "immediately [start] exchanging ideas … Richard was introduced to the Utica Steam Engine & Boiler Works … [He] had been working in wood, plastics, resins and so forth, and was enthusiastic at being able to work in steel. At that time the only fabricating company available was not a hands-on operation and expensive."[5]

Once aware of the Boiler Works and its tool crib, Friedberg quickly approached von Bergen with a proposal. "He asked me if I would mind having other artists working there," von Bergen recalls. "I said it would be fine, and they could help with the rent, almost jokingly, as the rent was $45 a month." Friedberg had alternative plans. He was acquainted with several key members associated with the New York State Council on the Arts (NYSCA), including Richard Kubiak, who was teaching at the State University College at Oneonta, NY, and the art historian and critic Irving Sandler, and was encouraged to apply to the council for money to support a studio of invited artists in

CHARLIE FISHER

Sculpture Space co-founder, c. 1982
Photograph by Sylvia de Swaan

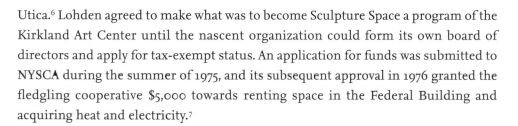

Utica.[6] Lohden agreed to make what was to become Sculpture Space a program of the Kirkland Art Center until the nascent organization could form its own board of directors and apply for tax-exempt status. An application for funds was submitted to NYSCA during the summer of 1975, and its subsequent approval in 1976 granted the fledgling cooperative $5,000 towards renting space in the Federal Building and acquiring heat and electricity.[7]

It was not long before the public was alerted to this promising venture. An article appearing in February 1976 in Utica's *Sunday Observer-Dispatch* reported that during the previous fall a group of sculptors had moved into the Federal Building and had begun to produce large-scale, modern steel sculpture. The reporter added, "They call their project 'Sculpture Space at the Utica Steam Engine & Boiler Works.'"[8] This initial group of residents included von Bergen, Friedberg and Fisher as well as James Iritani, another Utica sculptor whose legacy includes a sculpture that stands today at the Munson-Williams-Proctor Arts Institute.

It often has been stated that the early personality of Sculpture Space was formed by the types of functions permitted by the amenities of the Boiler Works. Among its inventory was "a 300-ton brake to bend steel, two sets of plate rolls to make curves, shears to slice through half-inch metal, a hammer mill, drill press, [and] the forge."[9] Sculptors could gain access to this specialized equipment at prices roughly one-third of what they would expect to pay in big-city facilities. The coincidence of materials

JOHN VON BERGEN
Sculpture Space co-founder
In his studio, 2004
Courtesy of the artist

[top, left]

RICHARD FRIEDBERG
Sculpture Space co-founder
In his studio, 2004
Courtesy of the artist
Photograph by Richard Walker

available from other industries and salvage yards in the Utica area also helped foster an environment uniquely responsive to the needs of large-scale steel sculptors.[10]

Ten artists came to the Federal Building in 1976, its second year of operation; 13 in 1977 and 12 in 1978. Among these artists were Isaac Witkin, William Tucker and Willard Boepple, all from New York City and Bennington, VT;[11] Del Geist, from Florida; and James McDermid, from nearby Rome, NY. The space drew sculptors who were attracted by a desire for hands-on experience with their materials and for the assistance of trained steelworkers who would allow the artists to "stand right at a man's elbow and say, 'Bend it a little more to the left!'"[12]

An observer of this early scene provided a vivid snapshot of a typical day at the workshop: "Sparks spill on the floor as a sculptor slices through steel with an acetylene torch. … Another artist examines the weld he just made on a work suspended from a heavy-duty hoist. Outside, there's the ancient sound of hammer and anvil as yet another sculptor labors over the live coals at the forge." This vulcanian vision is supported by another commentator, who describes Utica's "creative 'metal man'" as "more than just an artist. He must also be part blacksmith, part welder, part machinist, part crane operator, part torchman, and part strongman."[13]

Among the pioneer residents of Sculpture Space were a number of up-and-coming artists who were helpful in promoting the new facility through word-of-mouth. Willard Boepple, who created some 30 sculptures during a residency of several months in late 1976 and early 1977 for an exhibition at Aquavella Gallery, in New York City, claimed that the time spent in Utica was "the most productive and creative period of my life."[14] Del Geist was enthusiastic about the "great working space … [and] access to a vast array of industrial equipment and facilities with complete cooperation and support." The influential art critic Clement Greenberg, another early visitor to the workshop, added his imprimatur: "The Sculpture Space enterprise is almost too good to be true. But I've seen it and it works. Like a godsend for sculptors — and there are more and more of them — who work in direct metal."[15]

Despite glowing praise and a steady influx of artists, Sculpture Space scraped along during its first years. Bernadine Lohden, who continued her connection with the organization as a member of the board that was established in 1976, recalls that, even after the group's success at incorporation as a nonprofit organization in 1978, "there were a lot of downs and several meetings were held where the main proposal was to dispose of the program. However, it always was vetoed and we struggled on."[16]

Enter Sylvia de Swaan. Initially hired as Sculpture Space's executive secretary in 1979 through government money provided by the CETA (Comprehensive Employment and Training Act) program, de Swaan was a photographer who was at first reluctant to take on a full-time position that would leave less time for her own artwork.[17] After 18 months on the job, however, she found that she was "hooked," and she was invited to be executive director.[18] In 1980, she hired Jonathan Kirk, a young British sculptor, to be the group's studio manager, and they would go on to work in tandem as partners for the next 15 years. Stabilization and growth would come slowly but surely during their tenure, effected through the combination of their leadership, the support of a committed volunteer board, the increasing attachment of the city and community, a consortium of financial backing and the creative vitality of the visiting artists.

With de Swaan and Kirk, Sculpture Space took a prominent place among an international coterie of alternative artist spaces and residencies. The heart of their mission was shaped by the keen responsibility they felt to the community of artists who came to Sculpture Space to "experiment and grow in their work." They actively encouraged the participation of new artists, reminding them that "the studio is not set up solely for working with steel."[19] They made the timely decision to look at the definition of sculpture in its broadest possible sense in order to accommodate new ideas and materials. This openness was spurred partly by a sea change in the interests of the art world, which, by the 1980s, had witnessed many alternatives to heroically scaled abstract metal sculpture; partly by the recommendations of government funding agencies; and partly by the skills of Kirk, who was able to facilitate complex projects.

An emblem of this shift was heralded in a press release describing a one-night-only presentation by sculptor Mineo Aayamaguchi on May 2, 1981: "His performances ... are, in a sense, sculpture in motion. He uses no sound and creates a meditative atmosphere by positioning himself in the space in relation to found objects."[20] Sculpture Space soon earned a reputation for sculptural pluralism, and residents began to produce "quirkier things," among them site-specific installations, video and other photo-based work, and even objects produced on a sewing machine. Emphasis also shifted from the creation of a finished product to viewing the residency as an opportunity for two months of uninterrupted rumination and experimentation. De Swaan remembers it as "an abrupt change that happened gradually;" Kirk notes dryly, "Not all the works created here threaten to burst through the roof."[21]

The nature of the residency, and of the residents, was also experiencing change. At the

LEE TRIBE
Sculpture Space resident, 1979–1984, 1987/1988
Photograph by Sylvia de Swaan, n.d.

outset, Sculpture Space was open to professional sculptors who were asked to submit a description of their project, the amount of time they would need to complete it, and when they were available to work. The facility could accommodate three or four residents at one time and would host up to ten or so artists each year. Residents were not funded, but they could use the facilities of the Boiler Works, and many were housed at no cost in the homes of board members and volunteers.[22] By the early 1980s, though, the annual attendance was hovering between 15 and 20 residents, and a few artists each year were awarded funded residencies; by the mid-1990s NYSCA was funding a number of New York state artists annually.[23]

During the early years of Sculpture Space, few women were seen in the shop.[24] From the 1980s, however, they began to represent a larger proportion of the mix, and by the mid-1990s they often accounted for half the yearly residents. The program also attracted an increasingly international roster of artists, first from the United Kingdom, then from Canada and Australia, and later from Japan, Yugoslavia and Argentina. By the end of the 1980s the Netherlands, Sweden, Hungary, Germany, China and Spain were also represented by artists on site; and today a full quarter of the annual residents come from outside the United States.[25]

Notable accomplishments followed these early developments. In 1982, having been sold to the Heat Extraction Corporation, the Utica Steam Engine & Boiler Works declared bankruptcy, putting the future of Sculpture Space in jeopardy for the next few years. Then, in 1985, after many months of hard work and strategizing on the part of de Swaan and Kirk, the building that housed the workspace was purchased, for $6,000, at a city of Utica tax auction. Sculpture Space now owned its home.[26]

National recognition and awards were garnered, beginning with statewide designation as a "Primary Arts Organization" (meaning that it is an unduplicated concern that fulfills a need as no other facility does) by NYSCA in 1984 and the receipt of New York State's Governor's Award for Excellence in the Arts in 1987. De Swaan recalls that the community began to see Sculpture Space in a brighter light with the realization that "maybe Sculpture Space is important."[27] Any doubt would be put to rest in 1990, when the workshop was chosen as one of only 18 recipients nationwide of an institutional advancement grant from the John D. and Catherine T. MacArthur Foundation in recognition of its critical role in supporting the creative process for artists.

On the eve of the 20th-anniversary celebrations of the founding of Sculpture Space, Sylvia de Swaan left her position to pursue a long-term photography project, and in July 1995 the organization welcomed its second executive director, Gina Murtagh, who had been teaching photography and media at the Herron School of Art at Indiana University, Perdue, and before that, the assistant director at Light Work in Syracuse, NY. With the basic mission understood and the artists' program in place, Murtagh's efforts during her directorship would be aimed at ensuring financial stability and growth for the operation, increasing regional support and, especially, promoting board development.[28] She more than doubled the institution's budget through business sponsorships of annual fundraising events, and she pursued organizational improvements through entrepreneurial activities. At the time, as now, Sculpture Space's signature fundraiser was CHAIRity, its annual benefit auction. Established in 1990 to mark the organization's 15th anniversary and held each autumn since, it features a live auction of unique, artist-made and -donated furniture. Ten years later, and with the leadership of long-time board member Joseph Corasanti, Esq., an annual Mardi Gras party was added to the calendar, and in the following year 60 alumni artists donated works to the Triennial Art Auction, held on April 26, 2001, at the Elizabeth Foundation in New York City. The event grossed $50,000.[29]

In 1996 Murtagh began the tradition of a "Friends Campaign," drawing financial support through a regional year-end appeal; four years later she worked with the board, led by Sheila Smith, who had just stepped down from a term as president, and J. K. Hage III, to meet a challenge grant that would establish the endowment campaign, with an initial goal of $100,000.[30] Murtagh also sought to realize a modest commission for the organization by facilitating the sale of artworks made at Sculpture Space to collectors, businesses and other arts organizations.[31] She tackled other objectives through targeted grant-writing, approaching the Warhol Foundation for studio equipment; the Trust for Mutual Understanding, a branch of the Soros

TAKASHI SOGA

Sculpture Space resident, 2000
Sculpture Space studio manager, 2000–2006
Photograph by Sydney L. Waller
Sculpture Space archives

Foundation, for the funding of Eastern European residents; the Milton and Sally Avery Foundation; and the Community Foundation for technological support, including a computer, digital equipment, Web site and email, and for a professionally designed newsletter, *Sculpture Space News,* which debuted in the spring of 2002 and provides resident profiles and organizational updates.[32]

Murtagh maintained the long-standing emphasis on enhancing the artists' experience at Sculpture Space. By 2000, through a combination of funding from both NYSCA and the National Endowment for the Arts (NEA), up to 20 residents could receive funding during their stay. In 2002, with funds from the Community Foundation and the help of a consultant, she conducted an assessment survey of the artists who had visited Sculpture Space during the preceding ten years. The survey provided quantifiable information that enabled the organization to be more responsive to the interests of its visitors; for example, as the survey found only 20 percent of the artists were still using traditional tools, digital equipment moved to the top of the facilities wish list.

Murtagh confesses to an "urge to do exhibitions," and during her tenure two milestone anniversaries were marked by major showings of Sculpture Space's alumni.[33] The 20th, celebrated in 1995 and planned prior to Murtagh's arrival, featured three exhibitions of works by former residents: one at the Munson-Williams-Proctor-Institute Museum of Art; another at the Kirkland Art Center in Clinton, NY, and a third at SculptureCenter in Long Island City, NY.[34] In 1997 Murtagh organized *INTER/CHANGE: Five Sculpture Space Artists at Stone Quarry Hill Art Park, Cazenovia, NY,* which showed works by artists who were in residence in 1996 and 1997.[35] Also that year Sculpture Space purchased, for $100, the property adjacent to the studio on which Ann Reichlin's 1998 project, *Insert,* stood until its demolition in June 2006.[36] For the 25th anniversary of Sculpture Space, celebrated in 2000, Murtagh asked five former resident sculptors to revisit Utica and install their work in public spaces throughout the city.[37]

The organization's involvement with exhibitions goes back to its earliest days.[38] This was never a programmatic goal, however, and despite several notable exhibitions, most funding sources reinforced the idea that the focus of Sculpture Space should be on the artists' residencies. Still, artists and staff were alert to exhibition opportunities, and these have ranged from temporary installations at local businesses and institutions to participation in national events.[39] In an informal way, works by Sculpture

Space artists are often on display around Utica and the surrounding area, and every year a few artists go out into the community and produce site-specific projects.[40]

In the fall 2002 edition of *Sculpture Space News* Murtagh announced her decision to leave Sculpture Space to pursue other projects, and the board began a search for its third executive director. Sydney Waller, an arts administrator with expertise in developing small but far-reaching cultural organizations, took up the reins in April 2003.[41]

During a visit in early 2006 to Sculpture Space to interview Waller, the corner office bustled with a constant stream of board members and artists who were dropping off donated masks for the upcoming Mardi Gras fundraiser. The staccato rhythm of their convivial conversation was intermittently punctuated by the screech of a power saw operating out in the studio, inviting investigation.

In one corner of the workshop, Brian Caverly, a young sculptor from Queens, shaped a hand-held chunk of blue polystyrene with a box cutter, an industrial vacuum at the ready. He also employed a stainless-steel wire brush and a surfoam shaver to form his sculptures; the initial cuts had been made on the recently silenced band saw. Across the studio, Paula Toto Blake, from Argentina, worked with low-tech industrial materials, including rubber tubing and hoses, plastic fencing, roofing tarpaper and steel wool. With scissors and glue, she combined these media with found domestic furnishings to produce slightly menacing sculptural objects. Nearby, a sleek white Apple computer monitor blinked companionably from its place on a battered metal

[bottom, left]

STEVEN PIPPIN
Performance/installation in West Utica laundromat (detail)
Sculpture Space resident, 1991
Photograph by Sylvia de Swaan

KIM WAALE
Sculpture Space resident, 1996/1997
Photograph by Gina Murtagh

desk. Toward the center of the workspace, a formidable iron anvil, bolted to a large segment of tree trunk, resembled nothing so much as some sort of powerful ethnographic artifact.

"What's remarkable is that we've lasted and been supported for 30 years," Waller claims. "We keep going in all our gritty glory." She is referring, in part, to the consortium of local and national support that conspires to keep Sculpture Space alive when other alternative spaces of its vintage have closed shop.[42] Waller is "moved by how well it all works," from the camaraderie shared by the visiting artists to the efforts of local businesses, from graphic designers to lumberyards to hotels, to help out with in-kind support and to keep the prices down. She has found that all aspects of the greater Utica society — which is part of the Mohawk Valley — are supportive of Sculpture Space, from city government to area industry, from the local artists who donate their work towards fundraising efforts to the "honest-to-goodness working board" that Waller describes as dedicated, involved and generous.[43]

Waller consciously builds on the foundations laid by de Swaan and Murtagh, which includes maintaining Sculpture Space as an active founding member of the Alliance of Artists Communities and of the newer New York State Artists Workspace Consortium. Working in concert with newly appointed studio manager (and 2004 Sculpture Space resident) Patrick Cuffe, who follows Takashi Soga, an internationally awarded artist who continues the steel tradition, she maintains strategic support of and targeted interaction with the resident sculptors while simultaneously engaging

LIZZIE ZUCKER SALTZ
Community program for MWPAI docents
Sculpture Space resident, 1997/1998
Photograph by Gina Murtagh

with the larger community.[44] Currently she is striving to reach out to more emerging and mid-career artists, both in this country and abroad, and is looking to expand the underwriting of their residencies. Securing the support of the Geraldine R. Dodge Foundation in 2005 and 2006 to sponsor a New Jersey artist is one such early success. A Pollock-Krasner Foundation grant for artists stipends in 2007 is another first for the organization. Overall, Waller says, applications to the program have doubled over the past few years; in 2006 158 artists from 12 foreign countries and 32 states applied for the 20 spots, up from fewer than 100 annually prior to 2003.

Waller also reports that, through the ministrations of the local Community Foundation and the efforts of the board and of former board president Sheila Smith, Sculpture Space reached its first endowment benchmark of $100,000 in pledges and outright gifts in December, 2005, just in time for the kickoff of its extended two-year 30th-anniversary celebrations, which included a gala event and seven different exhibitions through Central New York.[45] At the same time, Waller is moving Sculpture Space forward, working closely with its board of trustees. Together they have formulated a plan that is focused, in part, on increasing public visibility and community connections and upgrading the residence facilities with additional private studio space and more technology.[46] With the acquisition over the last two years of two strategically located properties (the Mustard house in 2005, made possible with support from the Community Foundation, and the 2006 gift of close to an acre from Utica Plumbing Supply) followed by the June 2006 demolition of the Reichlin and the Mustard houses, the Sculpture Space team is looking to turn the long-held dream of developing a campus that includes new construction into a tangible reality.[47]

Waller is focused on state-of-the-art housing to accommodate the Sculpture Space artists. Once that project is up and running, attention may be turned to a multipurpose edifice that could house education and exhibition facilities, with additional space for the increasingly popular and successful annual fundraising events. With multiple structures occupying the lot off Whitesboro Street, Sculpture Space might well revive the appearance presented by the cluster of buildings that stood at its founding, united this time by purposeful, post-industrial activity.

Thomas E. Piché, Jr. is director of the Gibson Gallery at the State University of New York at Potsdam and a former senior curator at the Everson Museum of Art, Syracuse, NY.

ANN REICHLIN
Artist presentation to board of directors
Sculpture Space resident, 1998/1999
Photograph by Gina Murtagh

Sculpture always has been a demanding medium — both for the artist to produce and, although perhaps to a lesser extent, for the viewer to interact with. It offers its creator possibilities to express diverse ideas with a measure of urgency surpassing any other artistic means. Its three-dimensionality, which is, in its very existence, confrontational, as it infringes on our space and forces us to react not only intellectually but also downright physically, brings this special degree of exigency to the intended message. And whether the artist chooses to deal with purely formal issues, personal or social history, individual or group identity, matters of ecology and nature, human habitat on a large or small scale and the related theme of integrating architecture and sculpture, or new themes introduced by the advancement of technology, there are endless ways to express those ideas in sculpture.

According to *The American Heritage Dictionary,* sculpture is defined as "the art or practice of shaping figures or designs in the round or in relief, as by chiseling marble, modeling clay or casting in metal."[1] The name itself is derived from the Latin *sculpere,* to carve. Today that technique is only one among many that leads toward the creation of sculptural entity, no more important than permanent or short-term site-specific installations or the latest digital technologies that are crucial to much of the best contemporary works. In addition, although sculptors still make use of traditional materials — bronze, wood and marble, for example — they also use cast rubber, molds, all kinds of resins and plastics, fabrics of natural and man-made substances and light, sound, electronics and gases. Found objects, too, appear in an impressive number of today's creations.

Within the past 30 years there has been an explosion of sculptural manifestations, ideas and materials. The concentration herein is on artists who were part of the Sculpture Space residency program in Utica, NY, with an occasional digression into the territories of those sculptors who have been instrumental in shaping modern and contemporary sculpture as we know it today.

During these three decades, sculpture truly began to function in an "extended field," as prophesied in the famous last chapter of Rosalind Krauss's indispensable book, *Passages in Modern Sculpture.*[2] This could not have happened, however, without much intense, worldwide, experimentation. The selfless dedication extended to furthering sculptural developments by those visionary sculptors who established Sculpture Space in the mid-1970s: Richard Friedberg (resident 1975–1978), John von Bergen (resident 1975–1977), Charlie Fisher (resident 1975–1979, 1981–1982, 1984)[3] and other

CAI GUO-QIANG
Clear Sky Black Cloud, 2006
Black smoke shells
Variable dimensions
The Metropolitan Museum of Art, New York
Courtesy of The Metropolitan Museum of Art
Photograph by Teresa Christiansen

early members of the "Bennington Group."[4] They recognized the need for a space that allowed artists not only to concentrate and develop ideas but also to execute them. They knew first-hand that sculpture is costly and labor-intensive. Greatly aided by the farsighted members of the business community of Utica, its civic leaders, the art administrators and staff of the surrounding institutions and colleges and the energy and commitment of its first formally appointed executive director, Sylvia de Swaan, the synergy that evolved at Sculpture Space in those early years was crucial in both carrying the residency program through some financially difficult times and in guaranteeing its development and survival.[5]

For 30 years Sculpture Space has offered a place in which to concentrate and to execute work to more than 400 artists from a number of countries, all of whom have brought their unique cultural backgrounds and specific individual aspirations to the two-month residency program. Yet, in spite of its tremendous importance to such a substantial number of artists, Sculpture Space is not a household name in the art world. There is good reason for this: Sculpture Space has kept its independence from the trends of the art world; and the selection of Sculpture Space residents has been driven neither by fashion nor by the market.[6] Here is a place of hard work and dedication to one's convictions of excellence and courage of experimentation, where many an artist has a chance to develop a style and to become established — an opportunity that might otherwise never have come.[7]

The work of John von Bergen (b. 1939), one of its founders, explores the forces of nature with imagery suggested by the sea, the shapes of the human figure and the formations of the landscape. He gathers cast linear bronze elements reminiscent of twigs and branches into entities "suggesting three-dimensional drawings of volumetric objects intended to create a tension between abstraction and representation."[8] Similarly Isaac Witkin (1936–2006), a Sculpture Space resident in 1977, used cast elements in structuring his welded pieces. Born in South Africa, he studied at St. Martin's School of Art in London under the British sculptor Anthony Caro. In 1965, when Caro returned to England after a three-year teaching assignment at Bennington College, Witkin assumed his American post. This brought Witkin into the orbit of the seminal American modernist sculptor, David Smith, whose studio at Bolton Landing, NY, was nearby and whose influence is clearly discernible in the works of the founders and early recipients of Sculpture Space fellowships.[9] Although Smith died in 1965, shortly before Witkin came to Bennington, his legacy, and visits by Witkin and other Sculpture Space artists to Smith's studio — enabled by the

[opposite]

RICHARD FRIEDBERG

Oratorio, 1993
Aluminum, epoxy
13′ x 12′ x 12′3″
Courtesy of the artist
Photograph by Richard Walker

powerful critic Clement Greenberg, one of the executors of Smith's estate — were essential for the early years of the program. At Sculpture Space Witkin constructed his pieces from varied materials and found objects. In general he used abstract shapes in his work that combined form and process; he explored the concept of pouring liquid metal directly into sand, allowing chance to enter his work, and he achieved color through the addition of chemicals rather than the application of paint.

In his late writing Juan Miró, the Spanish painter who turned to sculpture later in life, posited that one day sculpture might be made of gasses. It no doubt sounded improbably fantastic at the time, but the formations of smoke floating above New York's Central Park in 2006, the work of Chinese artist Cai Guo-Qiang (b. 1957) and his installation at the Metropolitan Museum of Art,[10] are strong reminders of Miró's prophetic pronouncement. While steel fabrication was the driving *raison d'être* for Sculpture Space in the 1970s, from the earliest days artists also pursued the ephemeral and performative. Dariusz Lipski (resident 1992) and Helen Lessick (resident 1987) used gas and flame; Tomasz Domanski (resident 1997–1998) used propane fire and wax; Polish artist Adam Kalinowski (resident 2002) worked with balloons; Hiroharu Mori (resident 2002), who investigated elements such as air, temperature, humidity and energy as well as the parasitic relationships of humanity and its sense of natural place, created inflatables, as did Lee Boroson, at Sculpture Space in 1993.

The title of David Smith's *Tank Totem Series* (1952–1960) implies the exploration of the spiritual concepts of non-Western cultures, at first pursued by American avant-garde artists in the 1940s in order to free the work from the constraints of representation. At the same time the works in *Tank Totem Series* acknowledge the aesthetic growing from the utilization of the detritus of American industrial production. Smith used the ends of steel boiler tanks as a main component of the pieces, and used the industrial welding methods to build their anthropomorphic shapes. Due to their composition, materials and methods of execution, these were some of the most influential sculptures of the period. Smith was most notable among the artists who almost single-handedly restored the acceptance of sculpture after the interests in the medium waned during the hegemony of Abstract Expressionism in the 1950s. The movement was realized mainly in painting and drawing, as the spontaneity of a painterly gesture could not be translated into a sculptural form without the requisite speed and immediacy of the artist's physical engagement. At that point sculpture was considered a rather cumbersome relic of the past — as that awkward thing one inadvertently bumps into when looking at paintings.

[page 28]

CHARLIE FISHER
Cubic Minute, 1980
Steel
36″ x 36″ x 36″
Installation at The Picker Art Gallery,
Colgate University
Courtesy of the artist
Sculpture Space archives

[page 29]

JOHN VON BERGEN
Pi, 1996
Bronze, patinated
38.5″ x 33″ x 13″
Courtesy of the artist

[opposite]

ISAAC WITKIN
Tornado, 1985
Bronze
27.5″ x 32″ x 24″
Featured in Karen Wilkin's *Isaac Witkin*
(Hudson Hills Press, 1998), p. 73.
Private collection
Photograph courtesy of Nadine Witkin

TOMASZ DOMANSKI

Industrial Cave, 1998
Rocks, steel, water, fire
Variable dimensions
Created during Sculpture Space residency
Installation at Sculpture Space
Photograph by Gina Murtagh
Sculpture Space archives

Despite the fact that the great theoretician of Abstract Expressionism, Clement Greenberg, was dismissive of sculpture until the 1960s, the medium survived these injustices.[11] At the same time Greenberg acknowledged the formalist tradition in sculpture, a very different artistic approach entered the field with Robert Rauschenberg's *Combines* (1954–1964);[12] Jasper Johns' two beer cans cast in bronze (1960) and Andy Warhol's replication of a Brillo box (1964). Also in the 1960s Claes Oldenburg fabricated soft sculptures of food, and George Segal and Duane Hanson celebrated the figure in monuments to ordinary situations in life that later grew into public memorials to the heroism of the everyday experience.

While some sculptors explored the commonplace, others moved outside into the open spaces of the American West to celebrate its vastness, solitude and the American

tradition of marking and transforming the landscape. They created some of the most spectacular pieces that have appeared in recent history. The earthworks of Robert Smithson, Walter de Maria, Michael Heizer and James Turrell are among the most monumental achievements of contemporary art, reasserting sculpture in an un-precedented manner and, along with it, the belief in its limitless possibilities.[13]

Public sculpture, ranging from figurative to abstract to performance, is a core segment of the 30th-anniversary celebrations of Sculpture Space. The works installed in 2006 on the campus of Hamilton College in Clinton, NY, were selected by advisory curator Sydney Waller, executive director of Sculpture Space, as representative of the sculptural tendencies of today's artists, and written about by Deborah Pokinski, associate professor of art history at the college.[14] In a 2006 interview for Hamilton's

ADAM KALINOWSKI
The Sky Reaching Cube, 2002
Wood, latex balloons, helium
12.5´ x 12.5´ x 12.5´
Created during Sculpture Space residency
Courtesy of the artist
Sculpture Space archives

[left]

DARIUSZ LIPSKI

Circuit, 1992
Rocks, steel, water, fire
2.5´ x 40´ x 3´
Courtesy of the artist
Sculpture Space archives

[right]

PATRICIA TINAJERO-BAKER
ARIADNE CAPASSO
DAMIÁN KELLER

Green Canopy, 2005
PVC pipes, carpet padding, crocheted
VHS tape, plastic bags, speakers, solar panels
15´ x 10´
Installation at Hamilton College
Courtesy of Emerson Gallery, Hamilton College
Photograph by Richard Walker

Spectator, David Nathans, then acting director of the college's Emerson Gallery, which presented the Sculpture Space exhibition, states: "I want people to recognize that art belongs outside as a part of our everyday experience as well as inside in the often too quiet and too sterile environments called museums and galleries. I want them to be surprised and delighted by how different their everyday surroundings or nature looks when it is changed and challenged by a work of art. ... [It] is to present the juxta-position of the natural beauty of the north campus with the man-made artistic expressions, hopefully to enlighten, excite and even disturb the way we are used to looking at our environment."[15]

Historically, sculpture has been a celebratory medium, long used to commemorate events in both national and private life. From small votive objects to large equestrian monuments, these three-dimensional works serve to record specific and, often but not always, important events in a nation's history, to define its myriad ideologies and religious beliefs and, as well, to preserve personal memories.

Considering the profound changes society has undergone within the last century it

might be surprising that sculpture still serves some of the very same functions today. No longer based solely on the exploration of mythological, historical or religious themes, sculpture rises as a testimony to a different faith — that in the power of an individual, the power of commerce and the power of advanced technology, industry and the everlasting magnitude of nature. Daniel Buckingham's (resident 1998–1999) *Viewer* of 2006 is a case in point.

To create a sculptural monument that commemorates a specific event is still, nevertheless, a strong impetus. The pair of Vietnam War memorials in Washington, DC, created in 1981–1983 by Maya Lin (b. 1959) and in 1984 by Frederick Hart (1943–1999) is, perhaps, the most recent and best-known example. Lin's *Vietnam Veterans Memorial* integrates the long tradition of public monuments and memorials with the world of minimalist sculpture. Her simple geometric design, a polished granite V-shaped wall with the names of those lost in the war carved into the face, cuts into the landscape behind it, placing the viewer on a subterranean level. The simplicity of the monument, leaving the names as the primary focus, produces a very moving, solemn, experience. Curiously there was strong early opposition to Lin's proposal, and a year after its completion Hart's traditional figurative group, *Three Soldiers*, was installed nearby. What is remarkable, however, is how the general public has always preferred the dignified simplicity of Lin's monument despite its originally questioned, stark abstraction.[16]

Richard Serra (b. 1939) is known best for his often site-specific monumental, minimalist sculptures of raw steel that create a destabilizing dialogue of place and viewer. The scale and form of his sculptures require movement through and around them, allowing a constant reshaping of form as well as a continuous shifting of the surrounding space itself. The site-specific nature of his works, and his desire to incorporate the spectator's interaction, have made him a key figure in the creation of, and debates about, public art. Serra's *Tilted Arc*, installed in 1981 in the plaza of the Jacob K. Javits Federal Building in New York City, and the subsequent national controversy surrounding it, are evidence of the inherent challenges of art and, in particular, public art. The sculpture brought to a head the often-dissonant interests of the three main groups involved in any public work of art: the artist, the commissioning agency and the public. The public's strong disapproval of *Tilted Arc* ultimately led to its removal, closing one of the most hotly debated chapters in the history of contemporary sculpture.

Japanese artist Takashi Soga, who was studio manager at Sculpture Space from 2000–2006 and a resident in 1999–2000, also creates sculpture that is minimalist in sensibility and destabilizing in its effect on the viewer. His piece, *Silent Beam* (2001), embodies his long-time fascination with gravity and space, and his inherent questioning of our notion of stability. A 27-foot beam suspended above our heads "appears to float through its rectangular base, moving up and down to the effects of gravity."[17] Here Soga's work references the importance of Mark di Suvero (b. 1933) for younger artists working today. Di Suvero's imposing assemblages composed from found and/or prefabricated elements — beams, tires, chains, fragments of furniture and other materials — are poised asymmetrically, displaying disconcerting imbalance. The monumental scale of these almost aggressively expressive compositions — which can be found in many locations around the globe — turned di Suvero into one of the most recognized contemporary sculptors.

Perhaps the most widely known and discussed public projects of the past 30 years are those of Christo (b. 1935) and his wife and partner, Jeanne-Claude (b. 1935). Their massive-scale installations — such as *The Gates* in New York (1979–2005), *Wrapped Reichstag* in Berlin (1971–1995), *The Umbrellas* in both Japan and California (1984–1991) and *Surrounded Islands, Biscayne Bay, Greater Miami, Florida* (1980–1983) — are one-time-only projects that both play off and complement their carefully chosen locales.

DANIEL BRUCE
Assembled by Desire, 2005
Neon, aluminum, wood, epoxy resin, oil paint
47″ x 26″ x 38″
Photograph courtesy of the artist

ANN REICHLIN

Insert, 1998

Stainless steel and wood

16′ x 8′ x 2′

Created during Sculpture Space residency

Photograph courtesy of the artist

[above, right]

TAKASHI SOGA

Silent Beam, 2001

Painted steel, lead

11′ x 27.25′ x 11.6′

Installation at Hamilton College

Courtesy of Emerson Gallery, Hamilton College

Photograph by Richard Walker

Although these works are some of the most visible examples of public art, and although the creation of such projects forcefully alters and intrudes upon the environment in which they are installed, they have never been subject to the same outcries as other forms of public art. This is, in fact, because they are funded neither by the public nor by private commissions. Christo and Jeanne-Claude do not accept such financial backing, as they believe that it could compromise their art. Instead, they fund their installations with the sale of the documenting works on paper. Whereas the public's outrage regarding a work of art such as Serra's *Tilted Arc* was fueled in part by its having been funded by government money and installed in front of a federal building, Christo and Jeanne-Claude's projects are not subject to the same criticism. They are not permanent, even though they involve miles of space, surround entire buildings or islands and in fact alter the fundamental look and function of their surroundings. They are as much about urban planning and architecture as they are about sculpture, and they encompass the colors and design of painting.

In a similar vein, Sculpture Space resident (1998–1999) Ann Reichlin has created three interconnected site-specific works on the property of Sculpture Space: *Insert*, built in 1998, was a stainless steel wall that penetrated an abandoned house; *Solitary View*, of 2001, explored the interior of that house. The house was demolished in 2006 and she is now at work on *Translucent Home*, which will occupy the foundation. According to Reichlin, the three works "use the house as a metaphor for fragility, transience and continuance," and they "embody ideas of transformation, questioning the notion that a house once built is done, or site work once resolved is complete. ... They directly engage the site: the form is determined by the site and the meaning of the site is transformed by the work."[18]

[below, right]
ANDREA COHEN
Mist Over Lake Miami, 2003
Mixed media
7′ 2″ x 4′ x 5′ 3″
Courtesy of the artist
Photograph by Bill Orcutt

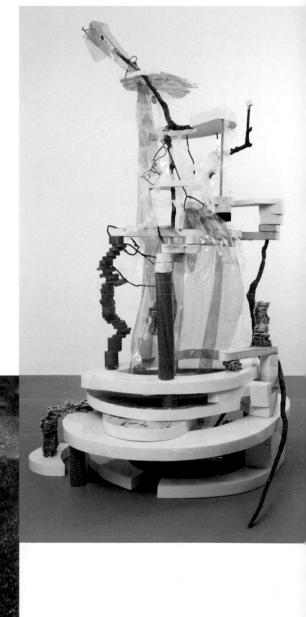

In a different manner, Claudia Vieira (resident 2004–2005) fundamentally altered the physical reality of her enclosed space by obsessively tracing a network of curvilinear parallel black lines on the floor, walls and ceiling, spilling outside her workspace and visually obliterating and redefining the physical space. Yoko Ohashi (resident 2002–2003) quietly transformed the same space with a subtle ribbon of eyelashes inserted in a crack in the concrete floor, while U.K. artist Jaimini Patel (resident 2006) altered the project room with dozens of suspended copper wires pinned from the top of the door to the corners of the room, radiating and audibly resonating each time the door opened.

Color plays a vital part in the work of 1993 resident Lee Boroson (b. 1963). At that time Boroson was developing his use of fabric as a sculptural material with which he created, until very recently, enigmatic objects and environments. In *Skinless* he connects elongated ovoids with a hose that fills them with water. Strangely evocative of simplified personages, they are placed throughout the large area of a park. The bright red color intensifies their startling presence. In *Sit' n' Sweat,* also of 1993, the red shapes are placed inside an enclosure of white fabric, reminiscent of infants' beds, which makes them appear even more anthropomorphic.

Because of its proximity to Empire Recycling, the now-closed Doyle Hardware and Utica Cutlery, three Utica businesses with a close relationship to its residency program, Sculpture Space has been able, especially in the earlier days, to help its artists acquire a constant and varied supply of materials. Peter Bowyer (resident 1981–1984; 1991–1992) relied both on Empire Recycling and Doyle Hardware for his materials; Wang Po Shu (resident 1990) used hundreds of forks from Utica Cutlery and Empire Recycling for the piece he installed at Sculpture Space. The perforated steel in the work of Patrick Cuffe (resident 2004) is also from Empire.[19] Andrea Cohen, too, a resident in 2004, works with available supplies to create constructions that explore not only the three-dimensional qualities of sculpture but also its possible connection to pictorial found objects. The bright pastels of her native Miami contribute to the layered meaning in her current work.

Another influential contemporary sculptor is Siah Armajani (b. 1939) a master of integrating architectural and sculptural elements. He frequently borrows forms and materials from vernacular architecture to build structures that function as contemplative spaces. Often he imbues his work with the narrative content that becomes discernible while physically exploring the space around it. The politics of space that are inherently present, although frequently concealed, in every man-made structure are often revealed in the titles of Armajani's pieces, such as in that of his 1992 *Gazebo*

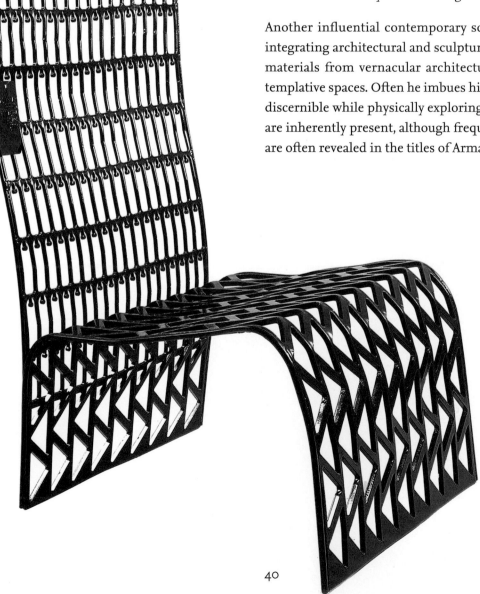

PATRICK CUFFE

Negative Space, 2006
Powdered coated steel
48″ x 22″ x 30″
Earth Day Art Collection:
Collection of Empire Recycling
Courtesy of Sculpture Space
Photograph by Michael LaPolla

for Two Anarchists: Gabriella Antolini and Alberto Antolini created for the Storm King Art Center in Mountainville, NY. Emerging artist Diana Al-Hadid (resident 2006) uses architectural forms as icons in her sculpture. In her 2006 work, *Spun of the Limits of my Lonely Waltz,* she created an upside-down Gothic cathedral whose blueprint is based on the footprints of the waltz and which serves to combine and confound cultural histories, blending beliefs of her native Arabic heritage with reference to Western architecture. In turning the cathedral upside down, the historical monument is destabilized and attention is reversed to the earth, away from the heavens.

In 2002 sculptor/architect Karl Jensen (b. 1964), a Sculpture Space resident in 2000, created *Pulpit,* a 25-foot-high sculpture/edifice. Trained as an architect, Jensen's construction can be entered and climbed upon. It has the word "pulpit" inscribed on

WANG PO SHU
Untitled, 1991
Cutlery
7′ x 21′ x 6″
Created during Sculpture Space residency
Photograph by Sylvia de Swaan

DIANA AL-HADID

Spun of the Limits of my Lonely Waltz, 2006
Wood, polystyrene, plaster, paint
64″ x 64″ x 72″
Created during Sculpture Space residency
Private collection
Courtesy of the artist
Sculpture Space archives

the sides of large plates that can be folded; many of the elements of the piece are movable. Not only does the sculpture serve as a pulpit, it also represents an amazing phantasmagoria of the most unexpected juxtapositions of shapes and materials, geometric and biomorphic alike.

Similarly, DeWitt Godfrey (b. 1960; resident 1981 and 1988) creates complex monumental sculptures by welding together metal strips and letting them react to the pressures of their own weight, as evident in his *Well* of 2006. His constructions are contradictions: imposing yet slouchy; substantial yet insubstantial; monumental yet fragile. And they contain architectural references suggesting, perhaps, the biomorphic habitats of the future.

[page 43]

[page 43]

KARL JENSEN

Pulpit, 2002

Aluminum, steel, bronze, neoprene,

plastic, concrete, ceramics and paint

70″ x 136″ x 297″

Photograph by Lydia Gould Bessler

[above, left]

RACHEL HARRISON

Sphinx (rear view), 2002

Mixed media

96″ x 48″ x 65″

Courtesy Greene Naftali, New York

The use of architectural space is also at the core of the work of Isidro Blasco (b. 1962; resident 1998–1999), a Spanish-born sculptor and architect who came to Sculpture Space soon after his arrival in the United States. He remembers the harsh Utica winter, so unlike those in Spain, as well as the difficulties of a foreign language and culture. "I had to work my way into this other culture, and figure out everything that I should figure out as an immigrant and as a sculptor, and do it fast," he writes. "Stuff that lasted in my memory … were details of the building, the faucet in the bathroom, the crack on the concrete floor."[20] Blasco's work consists of his photographs of the spaces he lives in, which he then mounts on wooden frames of various sizes and assembles into freestanding installations that one can sometimes enter or, more frequently, observe from the outside. Through his integration of imagery derived from the domestic and urban environment and the use of common construction materials such as plaster board, metal studs and, above all, wood, the artist creates unsettling environments that explore the idea of architectural deconstruction.

Subversion of accepted structural principles is pervasive in the work of Rachel Harrison (b. 1966), an artist who creates distinct sculptural objects as well as large-scale installations. Often using common construction materials, some of her pieces include unexpected elements, such as the television set in *Sphinx* of 2002. The assorted imagery on the screen introduces the idea of change and motion bringing

multiple levels of meaning into an otherwise static sculptural entity.

Following a 1992 residency at the studio space program at The Marie Walsh Sharpe Art Foundation in New York City, where she began formulating plans for a large installation piece, Rosa Valado first participated in the Sculpture Space program in the winter of 1992–1993. "Sculpture Space gave me the opportunity to continue exploring large architectural environments within existing interiors," she says. "This work initiated a series of works where the sculptures become their own architectural containers." Valado returned to Sculpture Space in the summer of 2006 for an extended residency in order to "further the projects, exploring form and function in light-reflecting and transparent materials with interactive performance components."[21] The result of her second stay at Sculpture Space, *Octagon: Transition Between Heaven and Earth,* which she completed in 2006, explores the configuration of space, spatial movement and transparency to bring out the inner dynamic of the space. The work is a simplified model of a larger project that was submitted to the World Trade Center Memorial competition.

Garden imagery and structure as well as segments of real nature are also often included in the work of contemporary sculptors. A true master of this group is Meg Webster (b. 1944), who created the whole simulacrum of a complex garden setting at

[opposite, right]

ISIDRO BLASCO
Hallway, 2005
C-prints, wood, hardware
14′ x 5′ x 7′
Courtesy of the artist and DCKY Contemporary

[above]

BARBARA ANDRUS
Three Spheres, 2001
Wood, twigs, branches, string
c. 8′ and 10′
Photograph by Richard Barros

her garden adjacent to the Contemporary Arts Museum Houston.[22] Petah Coyne (b. 1953) and Barbara Andrus use plants, branches and other organic matter to create large-scale pieces and installations that are both indoors and out. Webster's elaborate floral pieces frequently exude sinister beauty.

Roberley Bell (b. 1955) credits her stay at Sculpture Space in 1994 with the subsequent direction of her work. While in Utica she completed her first "garden" project, which led her to study the relationship between domesticity and gardens, or to the built American landscape. "My new series, *Flower Blobs*, takes its cue from blob architecture," she explains.[23] "The forms really do not exist in nature, though they reveal themselves as natural forms. *Flower Blobs* grows from my landscape projects, the space where the artificial meets the real."[24]

Nature also plays a defining role in the work of Emilie Benes Brzezinski (b. 1932), a resident at Sculpture Space in 1996, whose observation of and empathy for nature are the essence of her explorations of natural formations. Brzezinski's early objects, based on segments of tree trunks, were of cast resin. In the late 1980s, however, she perfected her current working methods and material in which large tree trunks are roughly hewn, by chainsaw or ax, and then positioned, often in a way that suggests a group of giant personages engaged in powerful conversation. "Each tree trunk has a personality," she states in the catalogue of her 1992 exhibition in Warsaw, pointing toward the anthropomorphic character of the work.[25] Brzezinski is one of a generation of artists, which includes Ursula von Rydingsvard (b. 1942) and Mel Kendrick (b. 1949), who explore wood for its physical properties as well as its expressive power. In their works the traces of human intervention are incorporated as important features — the struggle between nature and culture is the impetus for their existence. Similarly, James McDermid, a professor at the Munson-Williams-Proctor Institute School of Art, worked with both steel and wood during his multiple residencies at Sculpture Space (1976, 1977, 1979, 1987) throughout the early years of the program.

The work of Louise Bourgeois (b. 1911) is deeply personal and autobiographical. The vast array of media and subjects she has explored throughout her career are linked by her emotional and psychological history. Defying classification, her work encompasses single intimate objects, large installations venturing into architecture, pieces sewn from remnants of textiles, drawings and prints. All aspects of her work are permeated by her constant referral to the past and its effects on her (or, for that matter, on anyone's) present. Sexuality, gender, femaleness, family, vulnerability and strength

ROSA VALADO

*Octagon: Transition Between Heaven
and Earth*, 2006
Steel, aluminum
14´ x 40´
Created during Sculpture Space residency
Courtesy of the artist; Sculpture Space archives

ROBERLEY BELL

Flower Blob #76; Flower Blob #75, 2006
Painted fiberglass with plastic flowers, novelty
birds and fruit
69" x 21" x 14"; 65" x 14" x 20"
Courtesy of the artist
Photograph by RIT photo services

[opposite]

EMILIE BENES BRZENZINSKI

Spruce Echoes, 2005
Spruce
8.5´ x 13.6´ x 11.3´
Installation at Hamilton College
Courtesy of Emerson Gallery, Hamilton College
Photograph by Richard Walker

are interwoven into her emotionally charged pieces. Blending the physical, the symbolic and the anthropomorphic, Bourgeois' work represents some of the most unapologetically intimate and personal expressions of an artist's self.

Bourgeois' far-reaching influence affected generations of young artists, among them Cristin Millett, who created *Teatro Anatomico* while a resident at Sculpture Space in 2003–2004. In her work, Millett's intent is to "provoke contemplation on how we perceive, stereotype and stigmatize the female body and question the history that molded the controversy surrounding reproduction."[26]

Another young artist who felt Bourgeois' influence is David Baskin, who began a new body of work dealing with projection, film and installation while at Sculpture Space in 1995. "The time available to concentrate and explore new territories helped me tremendously," he states. "The fact that it is a small program helped to create an environment of friendship and a sense of creative collective purpose."[27] For Baskin, his residency was a stepping-stone toward further development of his work — work that investigates the memory of past acquaintances and family through particular selections of mundane objects grouped into special installations. "My recent work explores common objects we encounter every day, specifically within the domestic setting. Whether based on my personal history or on that of others, I am interested

DAVID BASKIN
Figure 54, 2000
Mixed media
Variable dimensions
Courtesy of the artist

[above, right]

CRISTIN MILLETT
Teatro Anatomico (detail), 2004
Mixed media
8′ x 19′ x 22′
Lightening and *Abdominal Hysterectomy:*
Dissection of the Observer
Created during Sculpture Space residency
Courtesy of the artist

in the transformation that occurs when these familiar images are re-contextualized within the artificial construct of a work of art. In this process, not only are the boundaries between personal and universal experiences obscured, but also those between memory and history and object and artifact are questioned."[28]

Cestmir Suska (b. 1952) also reveals in his work a special affinity for the exploration of the fields of memory as well as of the found object. Born in Czechoslovakia (now the Czech Republic), Suska's 1999 sojourn at Sculpture Space — his first experience working both outside his own studio and with other artists — was an inspiration. For Suska, who had exhausted the possibilities of his previous preoccupation with large-scale wooden pieces, the Sculpture Space studio, with its excellent equipment for metal- and woodworking, generated new materials and new ideas.[29] During his two-month residency, which was funded in part by the Soros Foundation's New York-based Trust for Mutual Understanding, he created a series of wooden pieces that were shown in September 1999 at the Embassy of the Czech Republic in Washington, DC.[30] Currently he uses a plasma cutter to incise patterns from his childhood — those on a tablecloth, for example, or a motif taken from a piece of embroidery or from a swatch of wallpaper — into large metal containers, such as discarded propane tanks. The use of an industrial container and a stylized floral or geometric design led to the creation of multilayered sculptural objects, many of which have been placed in public venues in Prague and throughout the Czech Republic. Upon returning to the Czech Republic Suska found an abandoned industrial building close to Prague, bought basic equipment and established a studio space that has become a center for artists.

Childhood memories — in this case disturbing ones of death, destruction and war — are an essential element in the work of 1993 resident Lynne Yamamoto.[31] Her symbolic installation of 2001, *Resplendent,* which consists of beautiful, fragile shapes and materials, comments on life, death, spring and rebirth through images of fallen Japanese soldiers attached to fabricated cherry blossoms. There is a beauty and poetry to this installation, as it makes use of the Japanese cultural admiration for the magnificence of spring and nature to recall the deaths of the young men. As the title of the piece proclaims, their memory comes shining through. The work is rich in content and addresses multiple issues that relate to other works, such as that of Carrie Scanga (resident 2005) that explore themes rooted in recent history. Scanga's art "explores how primal human desires translate into personal fantasies and cultural nostalgia." The images in her recent work depict "how a girl sees herself when she imagines a fantasy." The girl is "at the center of these images, because they tell the tales of the developmental stage when she is the center of her known universe."[32]

Social responsibility and the response to the conflicts plaguing the world also charge the work of David McQueen, who while at Sculpture Space in 2004 added new mechanical pieces to his series *Minor Plagues and Lesser Events,* and of Marsha Pels, a resident in 1980 and 1981. For McQueen, the machines "re-present natural phenomena as mechanically constructed events. In their actions, they create snowfalls and thunderstorms but in their implications they point to the responsibilities and repercussions we face as a result of our more thoughtless cultural and political decisions." Pels' 2005 exhibition, *Booty,* at the Schroeder/Romero Gallery in New York City, is a direct response to the tragic consequences of the American invasion of Iraq in 2002. The images of the destruction of cultural artifacts remind us not only of war and devastation, but also that aggression perpetuates the circle of violence. The work of John Knecht (resident 1984) responds to the Vietnam years, while that of Istanbul native Ipek Duben (resident 1997–1998) documents displacement (an appropriate subject for Utica, a state refugee center) in her *Farewell My Homeland* of 2006.[33]

CESTMIR SUSKA
Spirale-positive; Spirale-negative, 1999
Laminated plywood
120 cm high
Created during Sculpture Space residency
Photograph by Chris Cirillo
Sculpture Space archives

The sculpture of Christy Rupp (b. 1949), a Sculpture Space resident in 1983 and 1984, is modeled after recognizable shapes of flora, fauna and bacteria, but with a sinister twist. However, *Hire Intelligence*, made in 1983 at Sculpture Space, sought to light-heartedly poke fun at intelligence-gathering during the cold war years; it was commissioned as a temporary winter installation for Dag Hammarskjöld Plaza, adjacent to the United Nations, in New York City. In her main body of work Rupp brings attention to the effects of global warming and other self-destructive human activities, showing mankind's capacity to bring about paralyzing mutation of surrounding organisms and the effects of bio-engineering, which creates mutations of living organisms while at the same time destroying a plant's ability to reproduce. "The environment was traditionally presented to us as a vast system of elements swirling around our bodies and our planet," she states. "As we look toward the future, fears of global warming and lack of clean water, air and food impact poorer countries first. It's like there are two planets: one is always much closer to desperation, the other is comfortably shielded by economics. ... By choosing to view environmental and sociological problems as fixable with technology, we ignore the fact that we are part of a system with a delicate balance."[34]

[opposite]
LYNNE YAMAMOTO
Resplendent, 2001
Individually blown and sandblasted
glass bell jars and hand-cut archival inkjet
prints of cherry blossoms
Variable dimensions
Courtesy of the artist and PPOW, New York

[above]
CARRIE SCANGA
Coronation, 2004
Paper maché, paint, paper, charcoal
30′ x 16′
Created during Sculpture Space residency
Courtesy of the artist; Sculpture Space archives

DAVID MC QUEEN

Storm System, 2006
Vibrating motors, plastic bags, various
electronic components
Variable dimensions
Courtesy of the artist

During his 1997 residency in Utica Kenseth Armstead began to use discarded industrial materials found in and around the city. He sliced inner tubes to create *Body Works and Inner Tensions,* a series of wall hangings that both anticipates his subsequent investigation of tensions present within social interactions and also emphasizes the political content present in all objects. Although today Armstead's interests are directed toward new media and video works, he nevertheless states, "The installations remain taut psychological spaces defined by a natural conflict between the handmade visceral components and the machine-made elements and technical parts."[35] In a similar vein, Alison Hiltner, a resident in 2004, uses a variety of machine-made elements in her pieces that are a blending of medical technology, consumer culture and a quirky sense of humor.

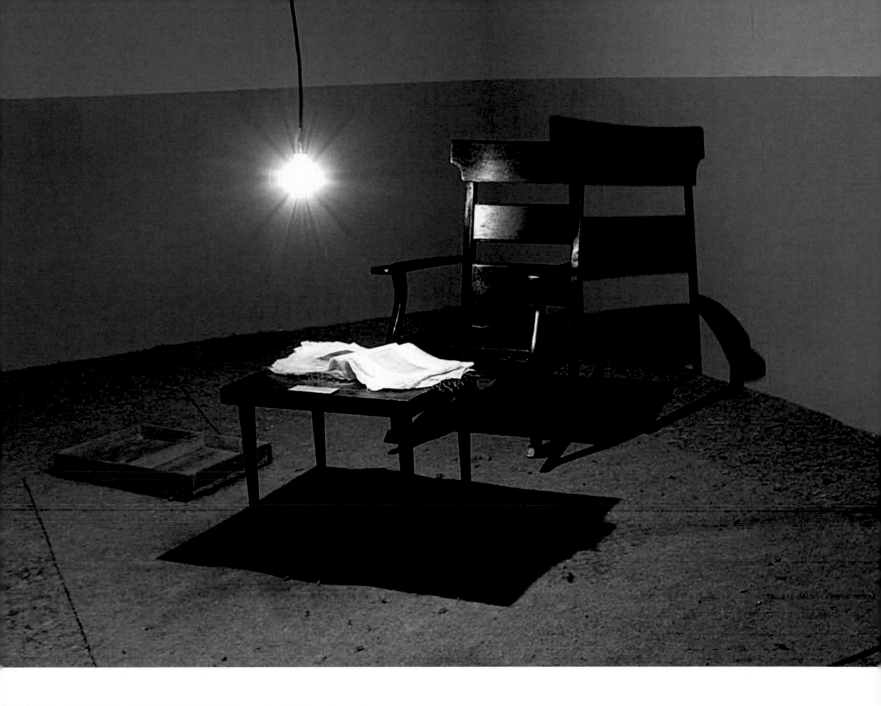

Technology is increasingly incorporated into current sculptural practice. Following the trailblazing achievements of Nam June Paik (1932–2006), who in the 1960s pioneered the use of video technology in art, numerous other artists realized the potential of material derived from electronic media. The prominence Paik gave to the television set in his pieces — he often used well over 50 monitors of varying sizes in his installations — reflects its ubiquity. This is well understood in the sculpture of David Kramer (b. 1963), who spent time at Sculpture Space in 1992. Kramer incorporates monitors in such works as *Cloud 9*, of 2001, that display videos from fitness shows woven together with his own videos of himself at work and play. Contrasting the artist's grand vision to pathetic realities is the constant theme of Kramer's work in video, sculpture, writing, drawing and performance. *Cloud 9*, he

IPEK DUBEN
Farewell My Homeland (detail), 2006
Mixed media
c. 20´ x 25´
Installation at MWPAI
Courtesy of the artist and MWPAI
Photograph by David Revette

ALISON HILTNER

Brain Protein Systems ... In Use, 2004
Altered Peugeot motorcycle, silicone,
parts from CONMED medical apparatuses,
aluminum, steel
Variable dimensions
Created during Sculpture Space residency
Installation at Spike Gallery, New York
Photograph courtesy of the artist

[opposite, top]

KENSETH ARMSTEAD

Surface Tension #7, 1997
Handsewn rubber and linen thread
48" x 60"
Collection of The African American
Museum, Dallas, Texas
Photograph by Jean Vong

[opposite, bottom]

DAVID KRAMER

Cloud 9, 2001
Mixed media
96" x 96" x 60"
Collection of the artist
Courtesy of KT+F Gallery (NYC),
BirchLibralato Gallery (Toronto),
Aeroplastics Contemporary (Belgium)

states, "is a sculpture about these contradictions. It is at once a sofa, and yet not big enough for naps or making out. The title implies a space of possible tranquility and reflection, but rather offers a preponderance of distractions and male fantasies from junk food to liquor to images of hard-bodied work-out girls."[36]

The most recent project of Simon Lee (resident 1992) is *Bus Obscura,* in which a passenger bus is converted to a multiple-aperture *camera obscura* using a back projection technique.[37] The windows of the bus are blacked out and punctured by innumerable holes. The *camera obscura* creates a 360-degree panorama of moving images inside the bus, and the passenger on the bus sees the real-time projection of the same scene in reverse. Lee also creates individual photographs of the images projected into the bus. Lee has presented the *Bus Obscura* in Miami Beach, New York City, Pittsburgh, USA; London; and Kampala, Uganda. In 2006, as part of a department of art residency at Colgate University, Hamilton, NY, Lee introduced the *Bus Obscura* to Utica with trips between MWPAI and Sculpture Space.[38]

A multi-disciplinary artist, Jane Edden produced two video installations while at

Sculpture Space in 2004. For *Colony*, she digitally manipulated raw footage of birds on telephone wires into a choreography, projected onto walls from which real wires extended from the same point and connected to the telephone pole in the video.[39]

Sculpture Space residents in the 21st century invariably arrive with their laptops, and their work often makes use of, or focuses on, electronic technology. Beth Krebs, at Sculpture Space in 2006, created an installation where light, apparently streaming through a miniature dollhouse-size window, cast shimmering reflections on an interior wall; David Bowen (resident 2004–2005) created an installation of inter-connected stalks of Queen Anne's Lace that, due to sophisticated computer pro-gramming, chirped whenever the air around them stirred; and Sterz, resident in 2004, projected natural phenomena such as falling snow on, or through, industrial objects.

The works discussed here represent a microcosm of the enormous breadth of

SIMON LEE

Bus Obscura (detail), 2004
Basel/Miami Beach Art Fair
Mixed media (1000 holes in a moving bus)
Variable dimensions
Photograph courtesy of the artist

contemporary sculpture as we know it today. Using past as well as present technologies and materials, this very elastic art form mirrors our present-day age of diversity. With today's globalization there is an even stronger need for artists to express a truly individual statement, using truly unique materials and methods. Sculpture is as powerful a tool as any art form through which an artist can achieve this goal. And indeed, the several hundred sculptors, all from different generations, backgrounds and countries, who have come together, if briefly, over the last three decades at Sculpture Space to think, plan and create are a singular testimony to the benefits of their residencies in Utica. Here, they are free to develop their careers at different times and in different circumstances, attesting to the constant need of such a place in spite of the ever-changing modes of the sculptural process.

Charlotta Kotik, the John and Barbara Vogelstein Curator and Chair, Contemporary Art, at the Brooklyn Museum, Brooklyn, New York, is also an instructor in the department of art history at the School of Visual Arts, New York. She serves on the international advisory board of the Soros Center for Contemporary Art, New York; and on the board of directors of The Adolph and Esther Gottlieb Foundation, Inc., New York, the CityArts Workshop, Inc., New York, and The Fund for Arts and Culture in Central and Eastern Europe, Washington, D.C.

JANE EDDEN
Colony, 2004
Video projection installation
c. 20´ x 25´
Installation at Sculpture Space
Courtesy of the artist; photograph by Sarah Lathrop
Sculpture Space archives

[pages 60/61]

SATORU TAKAHASHI
Dumping Sight: Landscape/Landscope, 1996
Plexiglas, water, mirror, steel, slide projector
24´ x 24´ x 11´
Created during Sculpture Space residency
Installation at University at Buffalo Art Center
Courtesy of the artist; photograph by Tim Philips

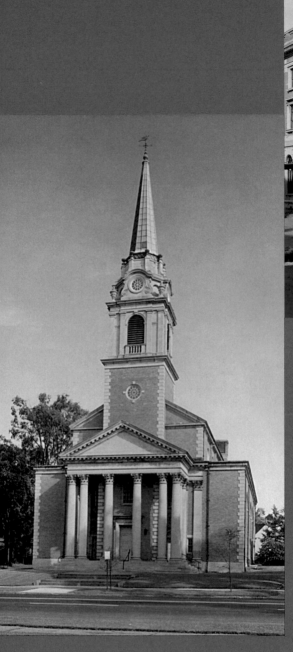

FIRST PRESBYTERIAN CHURCH
1601 Genesee Street, built in 1924

[top, right]

UNION STATION
Main Street, built in 1914
Photograph by Gale Farley

The successful conversion of a redundant industrial building to provide a home for Sculpture Space is but one example of Utica's resilience in adapting to major economic changes, a characteristic its citizens have demonstrated repeatedly over the past 200 years.

The history of Utica began in 1758 with the construction of Fort Schuyler to guard a ford of the Mohawk River. Bagg's Square, just west of the site of the long-vanished fort, marks the location of Moses Bagg's blacksmith shop and, later, inn, established in the years after the War of Independence to serve the needs of settlers moving west. In 1798 the Village of Utica was incorporated, its Carthaginian namesake reflecting the aspirations — and classical learning — of its residents. Two years later the New York State Legislature authorized the construction of the Seneca Turnpike (now New York State Route 173), which runs from Utica to Canandaigua linking with the Third Great Western Turnpike, and Utica's importance as a stagecoach stop was greatly enhanced. The original path of the highway coincided with what was to become, over the next few decades, Genesee Street, the city's grand avenue.

The village's economic fortunes received an enormous boost when the first section of the Erie Canal, between Utica and Rome, opened in 1819. By 1825 this technological marvel had connected the Hudson River at Albany with Lake Erie at Buffalo. Much of the labor used for clearing and excavating the path of the canal was performed by Irish immigrants, and thousands more Irish and German immigrants reached Utica by way of the completed canal. A generation earlier Welsh settlers had arrived in the Utica area, many of them settling on the estate of Revolutionary War hero Friedrich Wilhelm Baron von Steuben north of Utica near Remsen. The village grew in the area between the river and the canal, approximately the path of the present Oriskany Street, or the East-West Arterial. The North-South Arterial indicates the route of the Chenango Canal, one of the Erie Canal's many feeders.

When the first train station opened in 1836 it was the western terminal of the Utica and Schenectady Railroad. As the railways expanded, Utica's economic base became threatened, since many of those traveling by the new transportation system could easily bypass the city on their way westward. Forced to reinvent itself economically, Utica soon became a major center for textile manufacturing.[1]

Muscle-power for Utica's mills was provided by a new flood of immigrants, this time from southern Italy and Poland as well as Syria and Lebanon. The numerous churches in Utica reflect this ethnic diversity, and often within a relatively small area of the city one can find parishes that were once defined

as Irish (St. Agnes), German (St. Mary's), Italian (St. Mary of Mt. Carmel), Lebanese (St. Louis Gonzaga) and Syrian (St. Basil's). More recent houses of worship include Italo-Greek, Ukrainian and Russian Orthodox churches and two mosques.[2]

Fuel for the numerous mills in the Utica area was brought by way of the Chenango Canal, linking Utica with the Susquehanna River at Binghamton and thence with the coalfields of Pennsylvania. By 1870 the new Utica, Chenango and Susquehanna Railroad running alongside the canal could bring the coal faster and at a lower cost. By the turn of

the century Utica had become an important railway junction and, when the river was straightened and its channel relocated several hundred feet to the north to eliminate spring flooding in the Bagg Street area, the land formerly within the bend of the river became available for a 43-acre railway yard and a magnificent new station.[3] The opening of the wider and deeper Barge Canal in 1917 rendered the Erie Canal obsolete and, in 1923, the abandoned section that passed through Utica was filled in.

Yet even as the city continued to grow both geographically and in terms of population, its economic

UTICA LUNATIC ASYLUM
West Utica, built in 1843

[top, left]

MUNN-GREEN HOUSE
1 Rutger Park, built in 1854

63

SHAUN CASSIDY
Sculpture Space resident, 1998/1999, 2000/2001
Francis Xavier Matt II Endowed Chair, 2002
53.5″ x 20″ x 26″; cast cement
Photograph by Gina Murtagh

In recognition of friend and patron Francis Xavier
Matt II, the Sculpture Space board commissioned
Shaun Cassidy to create an Endowed Chair, sited in
"Boilermaker Park." The Matt family provided clothing
which embellishes the texture of the sculpture.

base again experienced major challenges.
Increasingly, the local mills felt the competition
from those in the southern states, and after World
War II the city's textile-based economy collapsed.
Civic leaders launched a "loom to boom"
campaign and sought to fill the abandoned mills
with high-tech industry, but the initial success of
this retooling was relatively short-lived and, for
the third time in its history, Utica had to devise a
new economic base. The city still searches for a
viable blend of new business ventures and
heritage tourism.

As the earlier immigrant groups prospered and
assimilated, waves of new immigrants arrived

with their special skills and work ethic. In the
generation following World War II a significant
number of Ukrainians arrived, and in subsequent
years political turmoil and economic injustice has
prompted refugees from Central America, the
Balkans, the Near and Middle East and South
East Asia to settle in Utica. Many of the trade skills
once supplied by Italian immigrants can now be
found in the Bosnian community.

In some ways, though, Utica has benefited from
its economic hardships. Although the misguided
and ultimately disastrous policies of Urban Renewal
in the 1950s and '60s left large areas of the city
center devastated, the lack of economic growth at

the time helped preserve virtually intact — at least until recently — entire historic neighborhoods that might otherwise have fallen victim to redevelopment. Utica's Scenic and Historic District, first established in the early 1970s, and expanded in the early 1990s, contains not only numerous buildings of exceptional architectural distinction, such as Richard Upjohn's Gothic-revival Grace Episcopal Church of 1856–60 and Ralph Adams Cram's Georgian-revival First Presbyterian Church of 1924, but also large stretches of Genesee, Oneida and Rutger streets that provide a virtually complete survey of two centuries of domestic architecture. At 1 Rutger Park the Munn-Green House, built by Alexander Jackson Davis in 1854, represents one of the masterpieces of the Italianate villa style. Another example of Italianate architecture is Fountain Elms, at 318 Genesee Street. Designed in 1850 by the Albany architect, William L. Woollett, Jr., for the Williams family, the house is today a part of the Munson-Williams-Proctor Arts Institute (MWPAI), housing its collection of 19th-century American decorative arts.

The Utica Lunatic Asylum (1843), now part of the Mohawk Valley Psychiatric Center, is one of the largest — and finest — Greek-revival buildings in America. Perched on a hilltop in West Utica, the limestone building, with 48-foot tall Doric columns that are among the largest recorded, was designed by Utica architect William Clarke, and its surrounding landscape by Andrew Jackson Downing. Examples of beaux-arts classicism are evident in the 1904 Utica Public Library at 303 Genesee Street, designed by Utica-born architect Arthur C. Jackson, of the New York City firm Carrère and Hastings and, on Main Street, Union Station, built in 1914 by Allen H. Stem and Alfred Fellheimer, also of New York City. Of more recent date, Philip Johnson's 1960 museum building at the MWPAI and Ulrich Frantzen's Kennedy Plaza Apartments of 1972 represent the modern movement of the mid to late 20th century.

The city's extensive parks system includes Memorial Parkway, a major link in Frederick Law Olmstead, Jr.'s early 20th-century project to encircle central Utica with a green belt. A dense array of outdoor sculpture, including Frederick MacMonnies' Swan Memorial Fountain of 1910,

can be seen along the parkway. In addition to the statuary and busts here and elsewhere throughout the city commemorating local worthies, there are monuments honoring the fallen of America's wars, the most notable of which is David Cunningham Lithgow's World War I Memorial of 1931, which guards the Soldiers and Sailors' Memorial Hospital on the campus of the Masonic Care Community of New York at 2150 Bleecker Street.

Works by several former Sculpture Space residents, including Mark Abilgaard, James Iritani, James McDermid, Wang Po Shu, Georgina Batty, Rainer Maria Wehner, Jonathan Kirk and John von Bergen, are sited prominently around the city as well.[4] If objects of discussion by some, they are objects of civic pride to most of the people of Utica, an inspiration to students and a validation of the professional aspirations of the artists.

The people of Utica are also fortunate to have access to a major art collection of American paintings, sculpture and decorative arts, which is housed in the MWPAI complex. Their cultural life is further enhanced by the Utica Symphony, the Chamber Music Society of Utica, the Players Theater — one of the oldest community theaters in North America — the Stanley Performing Arts Center and by several institutions of higher education.

In spite of its small size and struggling economy, Utica has much to offer its residents, not the least of which is affordable housing. Those of us who have chosen to live here delight in its ethnic diversity, its active arts community and the natural beauty of its surrounding landscape.

A Texan by birth, Rand Carter studied at Columbia, Princeton and the Courtauld Institute of the University of London. Before joining the faculty of Hamilton College as a professor of the history of art, he was a fellow of the Royal Institution for the Advancement of Learning in Montreal. In addition to his 16 years on the board of Sculpture Space, including two terms as president (1989–1992), he is a past president of the Landmarks Society of Utica and for one year chaired the City of Utica's Commission on Scenic and Historic Preservation.

[opposite, right]

RAINER MARIA WEHNER
Sculpture Space resident, 1999/2000, 2002/2003
Homage to Wayne Palmer, **2005**
Sculpture Space Endowed Sculpture, 2004
Galvanized steel, stainless steel
4´ x 6´ x 9´
Permanent collection, Utica College, Utica NY
Photograph by Larry Pacilio

[below]

JONATHAN KIRK
Sculpture Space resident, 1980–1991
Endowed Chair, **1999**
Roscoe Conkling Park
Photograph by Gale Farley
Sculpture Space archives

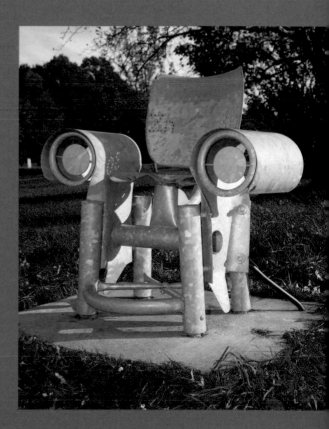

Arriving in Utica by train from New York City is like stepping back in time. The recently renovated Union Station recalls the early 20th-century splendor of the golden age of rail travel. With its classical beaux-arts features — polished terrazzo floors, soaring marble columns accented in warm, dark swirls, exquisite coffered ceiling and broad skylights — Utica's Union Station has welcomed visitors and residents since 1914. Designed by the firm of Stem & Fellheimer, whose work includes New York City's Grand Central Station, Union Station has been lovingly restored to its former grandeur. Across the street from the station, on First Street, is a hulking brick building that housed, until its recent closing, Doyle Hardware, a favorite haunt of many of the upwards of 400 artists who have been residents at Utica's Sculpture Space since the residency program was founded 30 years ago.

A ten-minute drive through the streets of Utica to the grounds of Sculpture Space reveals the changing face of this industrial city. Once rich in textile mills and breweries, the factory town where Frank W. Woolworth opened his first five-and-ten-cent store is just beginning to awaken from a post-World War II decline. Stores on Bleecker Street — a thoroughfare reflecting Utica's famously diverse population — while not offering the customary suburban quaintness of those in small downstate towns, seem poised nonetheless to provide the basics, from furniture and clothing to fancy coffees and pastries. Successive waves of immigrants — including Italians, Irish, Germans, Russians, Lebanese, Vietnamese, Cambodians, Polish, Somalians and Bosnians — have enlivened the community, introducing ethnic specialties in family-run restaurants, opening up small mom-and-pop stores and working in local businesses such as CONMED, a substantial global corporation on French Road that posts in-house information for its employees in six languages.

Formerly the site of the Utica Steam Engine & Boiler Works, founded in the 1830s as the Washingtonville Iron Works, the Sculpture Space campus is not a stereotypical artists' retreat. It does not offer the remote rural environment typical of such places as the Ragdale Foundation, Djerassi, Ucross, Yaddo, Millay or the MacDowell Colony.[1] Rather, the property consists of about three acres sandwiched between two well-trafficked local streets, one of which borders the railroad tracks. Here, the main building — a single-story, cement-block structure — incorporates the Sculpture Space studio, offices and a kitchen in a 6,000-square-foot facility, including 5,000 square feet of open space and two 400-square-foot studios for special projects.[2] Once known as the Federal Building, it was added to the Boiler Works factory to meet military production needs during World War II and abandoned some 30 years later.[3]

[opposite]

CAOIMHGHIN O'FRAITHILE
Longhouse, 2004
Wooden structure, white cloth, hay and twine
25´ x 4´ x 5´
Created during Sculpture Space residency
Installation in Union Station, Utica NY
Courtesy of the artist
Photograph by Gale Farley
Sculpture Space archives

In the early 1970s, while teaching sculpture at the nearby Munson-Williams-Proctor Institute School of Art, John von Bergen, himself a sculptor working in metal, became the first "resident" by creating a workshop for himself in the dilapidated Federal Building through a friendship with his student, Charlie Fisher, son of Morgan Fisher, then co-owner of Utica Steam Engine & Boiler Works. Von Bergen and Fisher cleaned up the building, moving the "body parts" remaining from the previous tenant, a tow-truck body manufacturing business. Fisher brought in some welding machines from the main plant and during the evenings worked with von Bergen and Richard Friedberg, a fellow sculptor von Bergen had invited for a short-term residency in the makeshift studio. (Friedberg, "the city artist," had a New York State Council on the Arts grant through the Kirkland Art Center, in nearby Clinton, to be artist-in-residence.) Together Friedberg, von Bergen and Fisher conceived the idea of transforming the space into a studio where additional artists could work, drawing on the resources of the Boiler Works. While Friedberg advocated for outside funding for the project, von Bergen and Bernadine Lohden, then director of the Kirkland Art Center, along with Charlie Fisher and a coterie of other supporters, founded Sculpture Space, eventually purchasing the building in 1985 for $6,000.[4]

In 1990 and again in 1995 the building was renovated and expanded to meet the organization's growing needs. Today large overhead garage doors open to accommodate easy access, large-scale works and to provide outdoor workspace. The building and grounds are used for work-in-progress receptions and special events. Inside, the once grungy gray-brown walls were painted a variety of shades of white — the volunteer efforts of students from Colgate University and Hamilton College, using paint donated by Golden Artist Colors of nearby New Berlin, NY — so the artists' work would show well. A wood-burning stove provides welcome warmth through the long, cold winters. An eclectic collection of industrial-looking equipment meets the eye: a fork lift, woodworking bench and a drill press, and an assortment of welders, hoists, band saws, sanders, grinders, and the like invite closer inspection.

It's 2006, and in this space four resident sculptors are hard at work — three of them in the vast open area and one behind the closed door of a private studio, a project room known as the White Room that is available by request to artists who need a controlled environment. By tacit agreement, silence pervades during this visit, although a small television appeared during the 2004 Olympics, NPR routinely reports on the war in Iraq and an immensely broad spectrum of music often is signed out from the Utica Public Library. Today, most of the artists sport headphones. The

BRIAN CAVERLY
Sculpture Space resident, 2006
Photograph by Sydney L. Waller
Sculpture Space archives

intrusion of a curious visitor goes largely unnoticed. Introductions are quickly made, however, and the residents describe their projects, at times expressing sincere affection for Sculpture Space and its staff.

Comparing his time at Sculpture Space in the winter of 2006 to his residency in September 2005 at the Vermont Studio Center in Johnson, VT, widely known as the largest international artists' and writers' community in the United States, Brian Caverly spoke of the freedom, intimacy and informality of Sculpture Space. Although he had his own studio at the Studio Center, he felt an obligation to engage with the 60 or so other residents during communal meals, lectures, readings and studio visits. At Sculpture Space, with only four residents, these activities are less formal and evolve more naturally. In fact, Caverly will visit Argentina next year as a result of a friendship formed at Sculpture Space. In addition, the $2,000 stipend offered him by Sculpture Space made it possible for him to be more experimental and purchase new materials for his work. Utica, he discovered, is a rich source for used furniture, which he has begun to incorporate into his sculpture. "I was living in Queens," he explained. "In the city, it is sometimes difficult and time-consuming to source my materials. Here, it is more readily available and more convenient to locate supplies quickly. So it does not take days and days to get things done."

Carmen Ruiz-Davila, a native of Barcelona presently residing in Cleveland, contrasted this residency to her recent experience at Skowhegan, in Maine. "Here," she said, "I am able to work on a large scale. Although the facilities at Skowhegan were amazing, this is one of the few residencies that provides both a stipend and studio space. This experience has given me time away from my job to explore. In Utica there are fewer distractions and there is tranquility to work. Skowhegan was very social. Here it is more serene. There is more time to think about my work and actually be more productive." Since her Sculpture Space residency, her work has changed. With the assistance of executive director Sydney L. Waller, Ruiz-Davila found local resources that might have been scarce in the rural communities of most artists' retreats.

Other residents during the winter 2006 season expressed similar enthusiasm for Sculpture Space. For Paula Toto Blake, the 24-hour-a-day accessibility of the studio space was an important factor "so," she says, "I can be here anytime and work as long as I need to." She values the time away from her responsibilities as wife and mother in Argentina to create art and explore new ideas in a supportive environment. In Utica, she found old inner tubes at Eggers Caryl & Corrigan, Inc., a commercial tire

AILI SCHMELTZ
Sculpture Space resident, 2005
Photograph by Sarah Lathrop
Sculpture Space archives

specialist on Oriskany Street, and colorful commonplace consumer products in the local Home Depot that have become key elements in her Pop-inspired domestic installations. Likewise, Melissa Vertosick values the "open-ended time" and a "welcome break from working two jobs and commuting three hours a day." Her visits to the Utica Public Library to research cameos resulted in *Ode,* a site-specific piece designed for the Samek Art Gallery at Bucknell University that references Renaissance paintings in the gallery's permanent collection.

For each of the artists in residence at Sculpture Space, the time and space for experimentation, abundance of interesting materials, access to specialized equipment and availability of the staff when needed make this residency so meaningful. There was praise for the studio manager, Takashi Soga, who assisted in countless ways to facilitate the artists' work and make their residencies more productive. A sculptor himself working primarily in metal, Soga generously shared his knowledge and expertise, helping solve problems and providing technical support when needed. He also transported the artists to suppliers if the sources were too distant for the bicycles donated to the residents by the neighborhood bicycle shop.[5]

Soga's predecessor, Jonathan Kirk, who served as studio manager from 1980 to 2000, fondly recalls his own experience and hands-on approach. "Sculpture Space stands out," he says, "because of the kind of service it provides. I loved the challenge of executing projects with the artists. It was endlessly invigorating. We would always say 'You can do anything here.' And we pulled it off."[6]

As a laboratory for experimentation devoted to the making of sculpture, Sculpture Space is entirely unique in the arena of residencies both in this country and abroad. In a recent interview, Sylvia de Swaan, the first executive director of Sculpture Space (1979–1995) and an outspoken advocate for the organization, said, "It is important to think about it in the context of the whole field of artists' communities. Since the beginning it has been part of a larger community that supports artists." Throughout its history, de Swaan points out, Sculpture Space has played a leadership role in the field.[7] As a founding member of the Alliance of Artists Communities, the New York State Artists Workspace Consortium and the National Association of Artists Organizations, Sculpture Space has long been involved in setting the standards of excellence by which such organizations function and adhere to their individual missions, supporting residency and workspace programs worldwide in their efforts to enhance services, disseminate pertinent information and assist fledgling resi-

dencies in establishing goals and fulfilling their missions.

Driven by a belief in the importance of the creative process in today's society, Sculpture Space and other artists' residencies, workspaces, colonies and communities make it possible for artists to work unhindered by the demands of everyday life. Among the residency programs that support artists who make sculpture, some serve primarily as exhibition locations for outdoor, site-specific work in season. Among these are Wave Hill, Socrates Sculpture Park, Snug Harbor and DeCordova Sculpture Park.[8] Many residencies are limited to summers only, while others offer short-term residencies of just a few weeks' duration. Sculpture Space, on the other hand, offers two-month stays year-round for each artist/resident.[9] Most residencies today are interdisciplinary, including writers, poets, musicians and composers in addition to visual artists. Sculpture Space is among the few residencies in the United States and abroad with a workspace program exclusively for sculptors. In addition, most residencies are in rural areas, making Sculpture Space one of a handful of urban artist-in-residence programs in the country with comparable resources for sculptors and installation artists. Others in this category include the Bemis Center for Contemporary Arts, Prairie Center of the Arts, McColl Center for Visual Art, the Isabella Stewart Gardner Museum, The Mattress Factory and Artpace.[10]

While many residencies in fact charge tuition and/or an application fee, Sculpture Space does not. Instead, it is one of the few that offers a significant stipend to all accepted artists.[11] Only Franconia, the Gardner Museum, Bemis, the Carving Studio, McColl, Roswell, Evergreen, Montalvo, Art in General and Smack Mellon offer somewhat comparable funding.[12] In addition, Sculpture Space is among a relatively small number of residencies that provide specialized equipment for three-dimensional work in metal or wood. These include Franconia, the Carving Studio, the Prairie Center, Ragdale, Kohler (which is funded by the Kohler Foundation),

MELISSA VERTOSICK
Sculpture Space resident, 2006
Courtesy of the Community Foundation
Photograph by Robert E. Montesano

[top, left]

EKKEHARD ALTENBURGER
Sculpture Space education outreach program
with T. R. Proctor art students, Utica, NY
Sponsored by Target in 2004/2005
Sculpture Space archives

Roswell, Yaddo, Bemis, the Weir Farm Trust, and Vermont Studio Center, among others.[13] Indeed, Sculpture Space, which has survived 30 years without both significant outside resources and a single fundraising source, lives up to its reputation as a kind of ideal community — a utopia, in a way, for contemporary sculptors.

There is, however, a certain irony inherent in the concept of Utica as a utopian retreat for artists. Utopian ideology, with its concomitant back-to-nature impulse, a characteristic that has spawned numerous residency programs and artists' colonies in Europe and the United States, developed largely as a backlash against the industrial revolution and the incursion of factories that enabled cities like Utica to thrive during the early 20th century. The first wave of artists' residency programs in the United States began in the early 1900s with the Byrdcliffe Colony in 1902, MacDowell in 1907 and Yaddo in 1926.[14] Established to give like-minded creative people — writers, poets, artists and musicians — time away from the debilitating heat of the city during summer months, these retreats were idyllic, peaceful and restorative. The well-known Black Mountain College, while not an artist-in-residence program *per se*, belongs

PAULA TOTO BLAKE
Sculpture Space residency, 2006
Courtesy of the Community Foundation
Photograph by Robert E. Montesano

philosophically to the initial wave of artists' retreats.[15] Founded in 1933 in the same spirit of utopian thought, it was a refuge for creative individuals and scholars.

A second major wave of retreats for artists followed the peace movement of the late 1960s and early '70s in America. Brought on in part by the desire to literally "retreat" from a society torn apart by radically divergent views toward the heart-wrenching war in Vietnam and violent race riots, numerous new artists' residency programs were founded. In addition, the National Endowment for the Arts (NEA), established in 1965, gave new impetus to art and culture in America. Public art projects began to flourish as well, heightening awareness of art in general, and large-scale sculpture became more visible in museums, galleries and public places. Among the residency programs that include facilities for sculpture founded during this period are Penland (1963), the Virginia Center for Creative Arts (1971), Millay (1974), Kohler (1974), Sculpture Space (1976) and Djerassi (1979).[16]

Artists, intellectuals and radical thinkers were among the founders of a successive wave of residencies during the 1980s and '90s. Some of these were established to preserve land or historic properties, thus avoiding harsh tax penalties or devastating commercial development; others, the Julia and David White Artists' Colony and the Prairie Center of the Arts, were established through philanthropic gestures by parents in honor of children who were artists. The Atlantic Center for the Arts, Headlands, Ucross and ArtCenter/South Florida were also founded during the 1980s.[17]

Since the 1990s, the proliferation of artist-in-residence programs has been due indirectly to cutbacks in government spending on the arts; in particular, to the elimination of individual artist grants once offered through the NEA. In response to this loss of NEA funding, the John D. and Catherine T. MacArthur Foundation awarded substantial institutional advancement grants to 18 arts organizations, including, in 1990, Sculpture Space, thus enabling them to increase support for individual artists through their residencies and programming. Sculpture Space used its grant to renovate and expand existing facilities, adding much-needed space and ensuring a more secure future for its residency program.

According to Caitlin Strokosch, program and communications director of the Alliance for Artists Communities, residency programs have stepped up to the plate, so to speak, in the last decade, helping to fill the funding gap for individual artists by contributing $36 million annually in the form of stipends, room and board, technical assistance and travel grants.[18] Sculpture Space ranks high among these. A large

AMOS SCULLY
Sculpture Space resident, 2005
Photograph by Sarah Lathrop
Sculpture Space archives

number of programs offer partial funding through fellowships or grants; others, including Art Omi, Millay, MacDowell and Yaddo, offer no-fee, or unfunded, residencies that include in-kind support such as room and cooked meals.[19] Still others actually charge artists to attend (Vermont Studio Center can charge as much as $3,000 if no fellowship is available).

Many residency programs are more highly structured than Sculpture Space, with regular schedules for meals, workshops and lectures as well as obligatory open studios, community service or outreach projects and other kinds of collaborations with local schools, universities and educational groups. As evidence of the growing popularity of community outreach programs, Strokosch points out that the traditional utopian image of the artist working alone in a studio in the woods is rapidly shifting as more artists become more actively engaged with the public through networking opportunities imposed on them by formal residency policies or as part of a volunteer program.[20] McColl, for instance, requires each resident to commit to two community outreach initiatives. For residents of Kohler, the time commitment is eight hours per month. The Gardner Museum encourages residents to commit to a 12-hour partnership with the museum's education department and local schools. Other residencies request public presentations, donations of artwork to local arts institutions or to the residency's permanent collection. The result, of course, is more awareness of the role of the artist in society and of the important role of residencies in building relationships between artists and the community.

Art Omi invites critics, curators and gallerists to visit artists in their studios to "help residents cultivate career opportunities."[21] Sculpture Space arranges curatorial studio visits from Mary Murray, curator of contemporary art at the Munson-Williams-Proctor Arts Institute (MWPAI), enhancing the individual careers of the residents and also strengthening the collaborative relationship between the two institutions.

Community connections have long been essential to the success of Sculpture Space. However, it has been evolutionary rather than mandated. Community outreach is voluntary at Sculpture Space and, as a rule, generously provided by the artists. School groups visit periodically, and although an artist may opt out of discussing his or her work with the students, that option is rarely exercised. In recent years both Target and the Mele Foundation have supported educational studio visits. Since 2003, during the city's annual "Utica Monday Nites," which occur from June through August and involve many local cultural institutions, Sculpture Space hosts an open studio for the community each week, at which time the artists may discuss their projects. Artists also lecture regularly at Mohawk Valley Community College.

The resulting relationships are mutually supportive and often have had lasting impact. Site-specific work is encouraged and, in many cases, artists ventured far beyond the walls of Sculpture Space, situating their work in public streets, an abandoned textile mill, and even Utica's treasured Union Station. London-based artist Georgina Batty constructed a flag of abandoned socks gathered from the local laundromat during her residency in 2005 and, with the active support of the mayor's office and the Parks Department, installed it temporarily in Columbia Square in the center of the city. Such projects require community support and commitment, which continues to deepen, making Sculpture Space a vital cultural force in the city of Utica and raising awareness of the essential role of creativity in the lives of its citizens.

The local library, historical society, schools, universities and especially the MWPAI have played supportive roles throughout the history of Sculpture Space. Mary Murray attends the work-in-progress open studios on a regular basis and occasionally hosts exhibitions of Sculpture Space artists' work. Lynne Yamamoto cites her Sculpture Space residency and 2003 exhibition at the museum as major turning points in her career. "I had at least three shows afterward that related to my residency and the people I met there, especially Mary Murray," Yamamoto recalled in a recent conversation. "A city in decline was very interesting for me. You sense a glorious moment. Memory became an important element in my work."[22] Daniel Buckingham, professor of sculpture at the Pratt upstate campus at the MWPAI, described his ongoing relationship with Sculpture Space. As a board member of many years and chair of the artist review panel, he is actively engaged in fundraising as well as in creating liaisons between the resident artists and the community. "We invite local sponsors to donate or help us acquire more equipment," he said. "Where we are missing a facility, we try to get the artist connected with resources, especially for multi-media and computer-based work. Munson-Williams-Proctor and Pratt have been particularly helpful."[23]

Local merchants and businesses have also provided much-needed services and supplies to Sculpture Space residents, simultaneously benefiting from their continued patronage. Doyle Hardware, a veritable treasure-trove of tools and materials, provided the basics along with more specific supplies. Caruso's Pastry Shoppe, on Bleecker Street, makes the cookies that are purchased every Thursday afternoon for

MAREK RANIS
Sculpture Space resident, 1996
Photograph by Gina Murtagh

the ritual "tea party," initiated in 2003, for residents and staff. Empire Recycling, one of the nation's largest recycling complexes, has provided inexpensive industrial materials and scrap metals for Sculpture Space artists since its founding. "We are the resource center for weird and unusual sculpture," says Steve Kowalsky, owner of the fourth-generation concern that celebrated its 90th anniversary in 2006.[24] As a symbol of its artist-friendly service, Empire Recycling displays a large-scale sculpture of a reclining woman by the "original" Sculpture Space resident and co-founder, John von Bergen.[25] Made from scrap metal collected during a 1971 Columbus Day celebration sponsored by Oneida National Bank & Trust (now Bank of America), the artist toured the city on a large flatbed tractor-trailer, welding his sculpture at various recycling centers set up by the bank. Today, it resides atop a railroad car at the entrance to Empire Recycling Corporation on Genesee Street. Most recently Empire Recycling has donated materials to Sculpture Space artists on Earth Day, which the artists then transform into art, forming the Earth Day Art Collection, which is auctioned off at the annual Autumn CHAIRity Art Auction.

As evidence of the vital role Sculpture Space now plays in the Utica community, funding sources for the residency have expanded over the years to include not only private foundations and state and federal grants, but also community-wide support from local foundations, business concerns and individuals. According to Waller, "There are numerous opportunities throughout the calendar year for local businesses to become involved with Sculpture Space, whether as special-event sponsors or as in-kind partners, to help bring a project to fruition. Countless individuals also help out, either as contributors to the annual fund or as volunteers who offer their time to make the aritsts' projects successful and their stay a happy one, or both. The public may also participate in special events, exhibitions and open studios. Today our community members, in ever-increasing numbers, are not only our supporters; some have even become enthusiastic art critics." Waller's predecessor, Gina Murtagh, who served as executive director from 1995 through 2002 and remains an active supporter, claims that "Sculpture Space is about process and an important safety net has been the focus of its mission and diversity of audiences served, starting with a working and giving board of directors." Murtagh also stated that up until 1998 only six New York State artists and two international or out-of-state artists were funded each year, leaving up to 12 artists without support. As part of the five-year plan at the time Sculpture Space then instituted full funding for all artists.

This year Sculpture Space celebrates its 30th anniversary with *Sculpture Central International,* a multi-faceted exhibition that features the work of professional artists worldwide who honed their skills during their residencies in Utica. Neighboring institutions have mounted exhibitions, hosted panel discussions and sponsored other educational programs in honor of Sculpture Space and its talented artists.[26] "Sculpture Space brings so much to our community," says Utica Assemblywoman RoAnn M. Destito, who frequently attends Sculpture Space events. "It encourages artists and sculptors from all over the globe to live and create here. Sculpture Space provides a showcase for contemporary art right here in the Mohawk Valley. I believe in Sculpture Space, its mission, and its quality-of-life role for our community."[27]

In the professional arts community, Sculpture Space plays a leadership role. Among the thousands of artists' residencies and workspace programs in the United States and abroad, Sculpture Space remains unique for its specialized service to sculptors. Here, artists enjoy the valuable gift of time to develop new ideas and bond with other artists with similar interests in an environment conducive to experimentation. Here, they have access to an abundant supply of resources and materials. Community support enables them to create and display large-scale work that might not be possible otherwise. New work develops and careers advance through this distinctive workspace program for sculptors that fosters creativity above all. With its dedicated staff and board, enthusiastic residents and broad-based community support, the future of Sculpture Space is, indeed, a bright one.

Margaret Mathews-Berenson, former editor of *Drawing* magazine, is a New York-based curator, critic and arts manager whose articles and catalogue essays have appeared in *Drawing, ARTS* and *American Artist* magazines, among others. A specialist in contemporary art and international cultural policy, she has taught at New York University, the International Center of Photography, Christie's and the 92nd Street Y, all in New York City.

DAVID BOWEN
Sculpture Space resident, 2005
Photograph by Sarah Lathrop
Sculpture Space archives

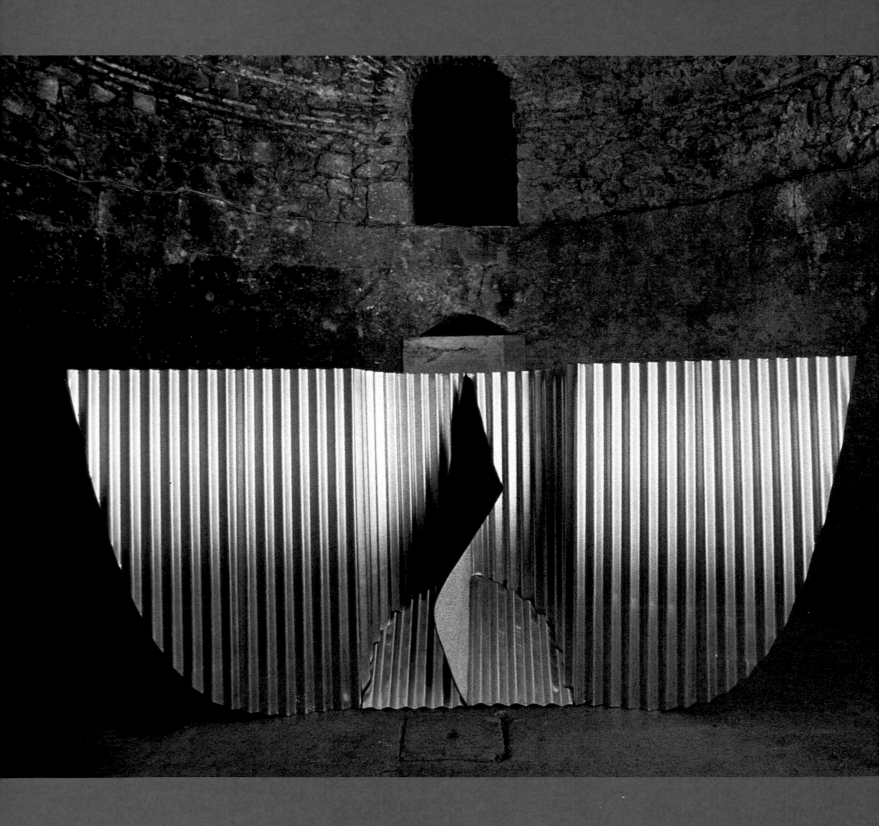

1975

CHARLES FISHER
Deansboro NY

RICHARD FRIEDBERG
New York NY

JAMES IRITANI
Utica NY

JOHN VON BERGEN
Clinton NY

1976

WILLARD BOEPPLE
New York NY

JERRY DODD
Waterville NY

CHARLES FISHER
Deansboro NY

RICHARD FRIEDBERG
New York NY

DEL GEIST
Sugarloaf Shores FL

DAN GEORGE
Poughkeepsie NY

JAMES IRITANI
Utica NY

JAMES MC DERMID
Rome NY

JAN PARDEE
Hamilton NY

JOHN VON BERGEN
Clinton NY

1977

WILLARD BOEPPLE
New York NY

CHARLES FISHER
Deansboro NY

RICHARD FRIEDBERG
New York NY

DEL GEIST
Sugarloaf Shores FL

DAN GEORGE
Poughkeepsie NY

BROWER HATCHER
Eagle Bridge NY

JAMES IRITANI
Utica NY

JAMES MC DERMID
Rome NY

WILLIAM NOLAND
New York NY

JAN PARDEE
Deansboro NY

TIM SCOTT
London UK

JOHN VON BERGEN
Clinton NY

ISAAC WITKIN
New York NY

1978

WILLARD BOEPPLE
New York NY

CLARK CROLIUS
Baltimore MD

CHARLES FISHER
Deansboro NY

RICHARD FRIEDBERG
New York NY

DEL GEIST
Sugarloaf Shores FL

DAN GEORGE
Poughkeepsie NY

JAMES IRITANI
Utica NY

STUART LUCKMAN
St. Paul MN

JOHN MC CARTY
Delaplane VA

ALAN PAULSON
Hamilton NY

WILLIAM TUCKER
(British)
New York NY

JAMES WOLFE
Bennington VT

1979

WILLARD BOEPPLE
New York NY

FRANK CITTADINO
New Hartford NY

JACQUES DAVID
Montreal Canada

CHRIS DUNCAN
New York NY

TOM FISH
East Stroudsbourg PA

CHARLES FISHER
Deansboro NY

DAN GEORGE
Poughkeepsie NY

BROWER HATCHER
Eagle Bridge NY

JAMES IRITANI
Utica NY

JOHN MC CARTY
Delaplane VA

JAMES MC DERMID
Rome NY

KEVIN RADU
New York NY

ROBERT SHEFFMAN
New York NY

KENN STEPMAN
New York NY

DAVID STOLTZ
New York NY

PATRICK THIBERT
Lambeth, Canada

LEE TRIBE
(British)
New York NY

1980

MIRIAM BLOOM
New York NY

BRUCE CLAYTON
(Australian)
New York NY

TOM FISH
East Stroudsbourg PA

JOHN GIBBONS
London, UK

CHARLES GINNEVER
New York NY

ROBIN KINGSTON
(Australian)
New York NY

JONATHAN KIRK
(British)
Utica NY

JOHN MC CARTY
Delaplane VA

RON MOROSAN
New York NY

ANTHONY PADOVANO
Putnam Valley NY

MARSHA PELS
New York NY

GABRIELLE ROSSMER
Stockbridge, MA

FRANK SMULLIN
Durham NC

KENN STEPMAN
New York NY

JULIUS TOBIAS
New York NY

DAVID STOLTZ
New York NY

LEE TRIBE
(British)
New York NY

WILLIAM TUCKER
New York NY

1981

MINEO AAYAMAGUCHI
Gunma, Japan

PETER BOWYER
Toronto, Canada

FRANK CITTADINO
New Hartford NY

BRUCE CLAYTON
(Australian)
New York NY

HANNAH COLLINS
London, UK

CHARLES FISHER
Deansboro NY

PAUL FULLERTON
New York NY

DAN GEORGE
New York NY

MARK GIBIAN
New York NY

DEWITT GODFREY
Kalamazoo MI

JONATHAN KIRK
(British)
Utica NY

MARC MANCINI
Utica NY

ALLEN MOONEY
Ithaca NY

MARSHA PELS
New York NY

KEVIN RADU
New York NY

BRIAN SCOTT
Toronto, Canada

DAVID STOLTZ
New York NY

PATRICK THIBERT
Lambeth, Canada

LEE TRIBE
(British)
New York NY

1982

PETER BOWYER
Toronto, Canada

PAUL CANFIELD
Ithaca NY

STEPHANIE FRANKS
New York NY

DAN GEORGE
New York NY

MARK GIBIAN
New York NY

RICHARD GOTTLIEB
New Paltz NY

ERIC EGAS
Leeds NY

CHARLES FISHER
Deansboro NY

JONATHAN KIRK
(British)
Utica NY

MARC MANCINI
Utica NY

ALLEN MOONEY
Ithaca NY

CARL REED
Colorado Springs CO

GIORGIO SADOTTI
(British)
Syracuse NY

RIC SNEAD
Tampa FL

DAVID STOLTZ
New York NY

LEE TRIBE
(British)
New York NY

1983

PETER BOWYER
Toronto, Canada

HANNAH COLLINS
London, UK

CHRIS DUNCAN
New York NY

DEBBIE FITZSIMMONS
Whitesboro NY

ANN GILLEN
New York NY

CAROL KINNE
New Berlin NY

JONATHAN KIRK
(British)
Utica NY

MARC MANCINI
Utica NY

STEPHEN PORTER
Bellefonte PA

CHRISTY RUPP
New York NY

GIORGIO SADOTTI
(British)
Syracuse NY

TIM SCOTT
London, UK

DAVID STOLTZ
New York NY

LEE TRIBE
(British)
New York NY

1984

PETER BOWYER
Toronto, Canada

JUDITH DAVIES
New York NY

CHARLES FISHER
Deansboro NY

CHRISTINE HELLER
Cooperstown NY

DAVE KING
London, UK

JONATHAN KIRK
(British)
Utica NY

JOHN KNECHT
Hamilton NY

ALAN LASAK
New York NY

MARC MANCINI
New York NY

CARL REED
Colorado Springs CO

CHRISTY RUPP
New York NY

DAVID STOLTZ
New York NY

LEE TRIBE
(British)
New York NY

1985

MARC ABILGAARD
Davies CA

TOM ASHCRAFT
Washington DC

"THE CHAMELEONS"
T. Grajek, K. Aoki,
B. Huot, H. Stahler,
J. Bruner, C. Saia

FRANK CITTADINO
Utica NY

LARRY CZASONIS
Clinton NY

DAVID GISLASON
Utica NY

REBECCA HOWLAND
New York NY

CAROL KINNE
New Berlin NY

JONATHAN KIRK
(British)
Utica NY

LES LEVEQUE
New York NY

MARC MANCINI
New York NY

RICHARD ROME
London, UK

VESNA POPRZAN
Zagreb, Yugoslavia

DAVID STOLTZ
New York NY

FUMIO TAKASUGI
(Japanese)
Erie PA

1986

MARK ABILGAARD
Davies CA

MARVIN BROWN
Berkeley CA

MATT CHINIAN
(Argentinian)
Diamond Point NY

DAVID GISLASON
Utica NY

LEANDRO KATZ
New York NY

BRIGID KENNEDY
New York NY

CAROL KINNE
New Berlin NY

JONATHAN KIRK
(British)
Utica NY

RICHARD LAYZELL
London, UK

ROBERT LYON
Baton Rouge LA

ANN MESSNER
New York NY

JONATHAN KIRK
(British)
Utica NY

FLORENCE NEAL
New York NY

SCOTT PFAFFMAN
New York NY

VESNA POPRZAN
Zagreb, Yugoslavia

MARY SCRUPE
St. Paul MN

HENRY STAHLER
New York NY

1987

ALAN BERLINER
New York NY

PAMELA BLOTTNER
Silver Spring MD

MARVIN BROWN
Berkeley CA

TRACY BROWN
Providence RI

ULISES CARRION
(Mexican)
Amsterdam,
Netherlands

CHARLIE CITRON
(American)
Amsterdam,
Netherlands

TERRY LEE DILL
New York NY

DANIEL DUGAS
Calgary, Canada

CLAUDIA FITCH
New York NY

MARK GAROFALO
Northford CT

KATARINA ISAKSSON
(Swedish)
New York NY

JONATHAN KIRK
(British)
Utica NY

HELEN LESSICK
Portland OR

LES LEVEQUE
New York NY

JAMES MC DERMID
Rome NY

MICHAEL MC KEOWN
(British)
New York NY

BEVERLY RESS
Silver Spring MD

ADRIAN SCHOORMAN
Amsterdam,
Netherlands

LEE TRIBE
(British)
New York NY

NICK WARD
(British)
Takoma Park MD

JERILEA ZEMPEL
New York NY

1988

MYREL CHERNICK
New York NY

DAVID EVISON
London, UK

CHARLES FISHER
Deansboro NY

JOSH GARBER
Toronto, Canada

DEWITT GODFREY
New York NY

JONATHAN KIRK
(British)
Utica NY

PETER LUNDBERG
Bomoseen VT

STEFANI MAR
New York NY

SUE REES
Bennington VT

ROBERT RYAN
New York NY

LEE TRIBE
(British)
New York NY

JERILEA ZEMPEL
New York NY

1989

ULRICH BAUS
Berlin, Germany

CLAUDIA FITCH
New York NY

JOSH GARBER
Toronto, Canada

RONALD GONZALEZ
Binghamton NY

SARAH HAVILAND
Buffalo NY

JOEL KATZ
New York NY

JONATHAN KIRK
(British)
Utica NY

PAUL LINCOLN
(British)
New York NY

LUCIA MINERVINI
New York NY

MOEBIUS PERFORMANCE
Boston MA

PETER MONNIG
Cologne, Germany

KATHLEEN O'BRIAN
New York NY

IVY PARSONS
(Argentinian)
Baltimore MD

VESNA POPRZAN
Zagreb, Yugoslavia

PETER SEBOK
(Hungarian)
New York NY

1990

CATHERINE BEBOUT
Fairhaven NY

JOSEPH CHIRCHIRILLO
Newark NJ

CHARLES CITRON
(American)
Amsterdam,
Netherlands

CHARLES DENNIS
New York NY

BETH GALSTON
Somerville MA

LOUANNE GETTY
Syracuse NY

SONIA GUISADO
Madrid, Spain

CHARLIE JEFFRIES
(British)
Paris, France

JONATHAN KIRK
(British)
Utica NY

ALAN LASAK
New York NY

WANG PO SHU
(Chinese)
Rome, Italy

EVE SUSSMAN
New York NY

1991

MAGGIE BEAL
Milwaukee WI

PETER BOWYER
Toronto, Canada

CHARLIE CITRON
(American)
Amsterdam,
Netherlands

DANIEL DUGAS
Calgary, Canada

LOUANNE GETTY
Clinton NY

PAMELA HELLER
New York NY

JONATHAN KIRK
(British)
Utica NY

DAVID KRAMER
New York NY

DIANE LANDRY
Quebec, Canada

NADINE DE LAWRENCE
New York NY

TASHI LEO LIGHTNING
Keeau HI

ANDREW MILLER
London, UK

STEVEN PIPPIN
London, UK

BEN SARAO
Weehawken NJ

GAIL SCOTT WHITE
Hamilton NY

1992

PETER BOWYER
Toronto Canada

CHARLIE CITRON
(American)
New York NY
Amsterdam,
Netherlands

BLANE DE ST. CROIX
St. Louis MO

JEANNE FLANAGAN
Albany NY

PATTY HARRIS
New York NY

CHARLIE JEFFRIES
(British)
Paris, France

WENDY KLEMPERER
New York NY

DAVID KRAMER
New York NY

MONIKA KULICKA
(Polish)
New York NY

LINDA LEE
New York NY

SIMON LEE
Bristol, UK

DARIUSZ LIPSKI
(Polish)
New York NY

PAUL MAUREN
Albany NY

PALLINE PLUM
Fishes Eddy NY

MIRCEA POPESCU
Bucharest, Romania

CORT SAVAGE
Hamilton NY

ROSA VALADO
New York NY

1993

ANNA BEST
London, UK

LEE BOROSON
Provincetown MA

KATE CHURA
Brooklyn NY

CHRIS DUNCAN
Schenectady NY

JOAN GIROUX
Berlin, Germany/
New York NY

SUSAN GRISWOLD
Portland ME

BENJAMIN JONES
Albany NY

ROBERT LYON
Baton Rouge LA

REBECCA MARTIN
New York NY

JOHN MONTI
Brooklyn NY

MARJETICA POTRC
(Slovenian)
Bethesda MD

MARSHA TRATTNER
New York NY

ROSA VALADO
New York NY

SHEILA VOLLMER
(Canadian)
London, UK

LYNNE YAMAMOTO
New York NY

1994

ROBERLEY BELL
Buffalo NY

SCOTT CAHLANDER
Baltimore MD

FABIA CLOSSON
Boston MA

MICHAEL
GRUENINGER
Syracuse NY

IMI HWANGBO
Waterville ME

WENDY KLEMPERER
New York NY

RICHARD LAYZELL
London, UK

LES LEVEQUE
Hamilton NY

WENDY LEWIS
Albany NY

BETH MC REYNOLDS
Snyder NY

TORY MENDOZA
Utica NY

ITTY NEUHAUS
New York NY

CHUCK OTT
Hamilton NY

JOANNA PRZYBYLA
Poznan, Poland

JOHN PUFKI
Utica NY

DONNA LEIGH
SCHUMACHER
San Francisco CA

1995/1996*

DAVID BASKIN
Brooklyn NY

CHRIS DUNBAR
Brooklyn NY

CHRIS DUNCAN
Canajoharie NY

ALVARO GARCIA
New York NY

EDWARD GIORDANO
New York NY

DOROTHY JIJI
New York NY

WENDY KLEMPERER
Brooklyn NY

LES LEVEQUE
Hamilton NY

JOAN CARLON
Cazenovia NY

MARGIE NEUHAUS
Brooklyn NY

JENNY POLAK
(British)
Brooklyn NY

JOANNA PRZYBYLA
Poznan, Poland

CARL SCHOLZ
Minneapolis MN

CAROLYN SPERANZA
Pittsburgh PA

ELIZABETH
STEPHENS
Jersey City NJ

SATORU TAKAHASHI
(Japanese)
New York NY

MARSHA TRATTNER
Brooklyn NY

ANNIE WEST
Brooklyn NY

1996/1997

MARCIN BERDYSZAK
Poznan, Poland

EMILIE BENES
BRZEZINSKI
(Czech)
McClean VA

ELIZABETH COHEN
Brooklyn NY

BRETT DAY
(British)
Pittsburgh PA

MILENA DOPITOVA
Prague, Czech Republic

JUDITH FLEISHMAN
New York NY

ED GIORDANO
New York NY

ALEXIS JAHIEL
Chicago IL

ROBERT KALKA
Brooklyn NY

STEPHEN LADIN
New Paltz NY

JEANETTE LOUIE
(Chinese)
West Orange NJ

PATRICK MC ENEANY
San Francisco CA

ERIC NELSON
Middlebury VT

MAREK RANIS
Wroclaw, Poland

YASUFUMI
TAKAHASHI
Tokyo, Japan

MICHAEL TALLEY
Brooklyn NY

KIM WAALE
Manlius NY

SUSAN WINK
Mt. Pleasant MI

1997/1998

KENSETH ARMSTEAD
New York NY

SYLVIA BENITEZ
Brooklyn NY

ISIDRO BLASCO
(Spanish)
Queens NY

ANN CHRISTENSON
Pullman WA

TOMASZ DOMANSKI
Wroclaw, Poland

RACHEL ECHENBERG
Montreal, Canada

LOUANNE GETTY
Utica NY

IRINA KOUKHANOVA
South Bend MI

SHAWNE MAJOR
Brooklyn NY

JOEY MANSON
Brooklyn NY

TIM MERRICK
Ithaca NY

CAMILLA METAL
Somerville MA

SUSAN MEYER
Boulder CO

JUAN ORMAZA
(Ecuadorian)
+
JEAN ORMAZA
Overland Park KA

JENNIFER PEPPER
Cazenovia NY

RENEE RIDGWAY
(American)
Amsterdam,
Netherlands

LIZZIE ZUCKER SALTZ
Athens OH

JENNIFER SLOAN
New York NY

ANDREA STANISLAV
Brooklyn NY

NICK TOBIER
Cambridge MA

JOSE VANEGAS
(Columbian)
Barccelona, Spain

VULTO
(Dutch)
Brooklyn NY

NICHOLAS WARNER
Rock City Falls NY

LI JIN XIAN
(Chinese)
Paris, France

AL ZARUBA
Baltimore MD

1998/1999

ULRICH BAUSS
Berlin, Germany

DANIEL BUCKINGHAM
Clayville NY

SHAUN CASSIDY
St. Louis MO

CHARLIE CITRON
(American)
Amsterdam,
Netherlands

TOMASZ DOMANSKI
Wroclaw, Poland

IPEK DUBEN
Istanbul, Turkey

MIKA EBATA
Tokyo, Japan

SUSAN GRISWOLD
New York NY

KARL JENSEN
Brooklyn NY

IRENA JUZOVA
Prague, Czech Republic

ROB LICHT
Newfield NY

VOJTECH MICA
Prague, Czech Republic

REBEKAH MODRAK
Columbus OH

BETTY NEWMAN-
MAGUIRE
Dubblin, Ireland

ANN REICHLIN
Ithaca NY

TONY STANZIONE
Brooklyn NY

CESTMIR SUSKA
Prague, Czech Republic

NOBUYUKI
TACHIBANA
Osaka, Japan

NICK TOBIER
Cambridge MA

TONI VANDEGRIFT
Wilmington DE

NICHOLAS WARNER
Rock City Falls NY

BARBARA
WESTERMANN
(German)
New York NY

1999/2000

LYNDA ABRAHAM
Brooklyn NY

MARLENE ALT
Minneapolis MN

GARTH AMUNDSON
Wooster OH

BARBARA ANDRUS
New York NY

MATT BLACKWELL
Brooklyn NY

ROBERT CALDWELL
Brooklyn NY

JAMES CHINNECK
Edinburgh, UK

REDAS DIRZYS
Alytus, Lithuania

VICTORIA FULLER
Chicago IL

JOSEPH INGLEBY
Glasgow, UK

TIM JAG
Berkeley CA

ANDREI ROITER
(Russian)
New York NY

ALISON SAFFORD
Boston MA

QUIDO SEN
(Czech)
Zug, Switzerland

TAKASHI SOGA
(Japanese)
Utica NY

JANE SOUTH
(British)
Albuquerque NM

RADHIKA
VAIDYANATHAN
Chennai, India

VULTO
(Dutch)
Brooklyn NY

RAINER MARIA
WEHNER
Berlin, Germany

MARION WILSON
Syracuse NY

2000/2001

CLAUDIA ARANOVICH
Buenes Aires,
Argentina

ISABEL BARBUZZA
(Argentinian)
Iowa City IA

DANIEL BRUCE
Providence RI

SHAUN CASSIDY
(British)
Rock Hill SC

STEVEN JOHN DAVIES
London, UK

GARTH FREEMAN
Alfred NY

CAMILLE GERACI
Rochester NY

WENDY HANSON
Seattle WA

TOMAS HLAVINA
Prague, Czech Republic

JAMES KNITTLE
Alfred NY

LUCAS MONACO
Long Island City NY

ROBERT ORTBAL
Oakland CA

DENNIS POTAMI
Brooklyn NY

THOMAS ROBERTS
Brooklyn NY

TASH TASKALE
(Turkish)
Syracuse NY

BILL WHEELOCK
Eden Mills VT

SUSAN ZOCCOLA
Seattle WA

2001/2002

MICHAEL BEITZ
Brooklyn NY

MATTHEW BURKE
Brooklyn NY

SAEMI CHO
(Korean)
Lexington MA

LARS-ERIK FISK
Burlington VT

PETER FORBES
Syracuse NY

ERIK GESCHKE
Baltimore MD

ADAM KALINOWSKI
Poznan, Poland

HEIDI KUMAO
Ann Arbor MI

HIROHARU MORI
(Japanese)
New York NY

MASANORI
NISHIMURA
Hyogo-Ken, Japan

PAOLO RADI
Rome, Italy

TIM SCOFIELD
Baltimore MD

BECKY SHAW
Liverpool, UK

PITIWAT SOMTHAI
Chonburi, Thailand

ISTVAN SZILASI
(Hungarian)
New York NY

2002/2003

MARCUS ALHERS
Baltimore MD

SHOHAM ARAD
+
MARK L.F. NICHOLSON
Fayetteville NY
Jamaica Plain MA

CARLO BERNARDINI
Rome, Italy

TIMOTHY BLUM
Bronx NY

BYUNGWANG CHO
(Korean)
New York NY

BEN DILLER
Davis CA

JESSE GOOD
Fairview NY

ULRIKE HEYDENREICH
(German)
Brooklyn NY

IANTHE JACKSON
Brooklyn NY

KATHRYN KENWORTH
Oakland CA

KIM MAYHORN
Brooklyn NY

LIZA MCCONNELL
Columbus OH

MIKE MCFALLS
Knoxville TN

KELLIE MURPHY
Brooklyn NY

YOKO OHASKI
Brooklyn NY

EDDY STEINHAUER
New York NY

PATRICIA TINAJERO-
BAKER
(Ecuadorian)
Boulder CO

RAINER MARIA
WEHNER
Berlin, Germany

2003/2004

ANDREA COHEN
Brooklyn NY

PATRICK CUFFE
New Hartford NY

JEFF DECASTRO
Ithaca NY

DEBORAH DOHNE
Syracuse NY

MAICA EVERS
Berlin, Germany

ALEXANDER GRAHAM
Nova Scotia, Canada

BRIAN GUSTAFSON
Bloomington IL

ALISON HILTNER
Minneapolis MN

PETER JOSEPH
Santa Fe NM

MINJI KIM
Seoul, Korea

CRISTIN MILLETT
State College PA

CAOIMHGHIN
O'FRAITHILE
Luimneach, Ireland

DAVID PARDOE
Brooklyn NY

HELEN QUINN
Brooklyn NY

MICHELLE
ROSENBERG
Brooklyn NY

HEDI SCHWOEBEL
Ludwigsburg, Germany

ALLISON WIESE
Houston TX

BEN WOODESON
Glasgow, UK

2004/2005

EKKEHARD
ALTENBURGER
London, UK

GEORGINA BATTY
London, UK

DAVID BOWEN
Minneapolis MN

STEFAN DORNBUSCH
Berlin, Germany

BEA DRYSDALE
(British)
Madison WI

JANE EDDEN
West Sussex UK

DAVID MCQUEEN
Brooklyn NY

DEBBIE REICHARD
Hopewell NJ

CHRISTOPHER ROMER
Brooklyn NY

KAORU SAKURAI
Saitama-Ken, Japan

CARRIE SCANGA
Cottekill NY

AILI SCHMELTZ
Portland OR

AMOS SCULLY
Rochester NY

STERZ
Burnt Hills NY

AIMEE TARASEK
Lowville NY

ALESSANDRA TORRES
Millersville MD

AMY TOSCANI
Minneapolis MN

CLAUDIA VIEIRA
(Brazilian)
Brooklyn NY

SAYA WOOLFALK
Scarsdale NY

2005/2006

DIANA AL-HADID
Richmond VA

ELAINE ALLISON
+
PATRICIA BRAY
Edinburgh, UK

PAULA TOTO BLAKE
Buenos Aires,
Argentina

BRIAN CAVERLY
Brooklyn NY

ABRAHAM FERRARO
Albany NY

JAYNE LAWRENCE
San Antonio TX

LISA LUKAS
Dusseldorf, Germany

MONICA MARTINEZ
San Francisco CA

MEGAN MICHALAK
Johnson VT

JOEL MURPHY
Brooklyn NY

RAY NEUFELD
Long Island City NY

AGATA OLEK OLEKSIAK
(Polish)
Brooklyn NY

RENEE RIDGWAY
Amsterdam,
Netherlands

HEATHER ROWE
New York NY

CARMEN RUIZ-DAVILA
Cleveland OH

ROSA VALADO
Brooklyn NY

KIM CARR VALDEZ
Rochester NY

MELISSA VERTOSICK
Greensburgh PA

AENEAS WILDER
Edinburgh, UK

2006/2007

WILLIAM BERGMAN
Albany NY

SUNGJIN CHOI
(Korean)
Brooklyn NY

CESAR CORNEJO
(Peruvian)
London, UK

CHRISTA ERICKSON
Stony Brook NY

CARLOS FERGUSON
Grinnell IA

RACHEL FRANK
Brooklyn NY

JESSICA
FRELINGHUYSEN
Princeton NJ

JANELLE INGLESIAS
Richmond VA

MEREDITH JAMES
New York NY

MICHELE KONG
Baltimore MD

BETH KREBS
Brooklyn NY

MANABU NAKANISHI
Osaka, Japan

JAIMINI PATEL
London, UK

PATRICK RENNER
Alfred NY

CLAUDIA SCHMACKE
Cologne, Germany

W. SCOTT TRIMBLE
Seattle WA

JINA VALENTINE
Berwyn PA

MARIA VELASCO
Lawrence KS

LUCIA WARCK-MEISTER
(Argentinian)
New York NY

KATJA KUBLITZ
(Danish)
+
RONNIE YARISAL
(Swiss)
Berlin, Germany

Sculpture Central International, a series of contemporary art exhibitions, projects and events to celebrate the 30th anniversary of Sculpture Space, featured the work of professional artists who were at one time residents of the program. The two-year series appeared at college art galleries, a museum, universities, an art park and two libraries, beginning in Oneonta NY, in February 2006, and closing in Cazenovia NY, in October 2007. The programs, located in central New York, had an international dimension, addressing aspects of contemporary sculpture: approaches and materials (Hartwick College); artists at work (Utica Public Library, Herkimer County Community College); art and technology (SUNYIT and Utica College); sculptors who use cameras (Munson-Williams-Proctor Arts Institute); and art inspired by nature (Stone Quarry Hill Art Park).[1]

FEBRUARY 16 – MARCH 21, 2006

Sculpture Space: Thirty Years in the Making
Hartwick College, Oneonta NY

Richard Friedberg, John von Bergen, Patrick Cuffe, Beatrice Drysdale, Aimee Tarasek
Sponsored by NBT Bank

FEBRUARY 17 – JUNE 1, 2006

Technology Radiates Art: Rainer Maria Wehner
SUNY Institute of Technology, Marcy NY

Rainer Maria Wehner
Sponsored by SUNYIT and The SUNYIT Foundation

MAY – OCTOBER 2006

Sculpture Space Inside/Outside
Hamilton College, Clinton NY

Roberley Bell, Emilie Benes Brzezinski, Patricia Tinajero-Baker with Ariadna Capasso and Damián Keller, Richard Friedberg, DeWitt Godfrey, Jonathan Kirk, John McCarty, Agata Oleksiak, Takashi Soga, John von Bergen
Sponsored by Emerson Gallery and the Office of the Dean of the Faculty, Hamilton College

JUNE 5 – AUGUST 30, 2006
and APRIL 19 – MAY 19, 2007

Work Zone: Sculpture Space Artists at Work
Utica Public Library, Utica NY and Herkimer County Community College, Herkimer NY

Sylvia de Swaan, Gina Murtagh, Sarah Lathrop
Sponsored by Partners Trust Bank, with additional support from Light Work Inc. and Seifert Graphics Inc.

SEPTEMBER 8/9, 2006

Sculpture Symposium: Public Art on Campus
Colgate University, Hamilton NY
and Hamilton College, Clinton NY
Speakers: Mary Miss, sculptor, film-maker, environmental artist; Wendy Feuer, consultant on public art and urban design, New York City; Harriet Senie, professor of art history, graduate center, City University New York; Alison de Lima Greene, curator of contemporary art and special projects, Museum of Fine Arts, Houston, TX; Richard Friedberg, artist; Patricia Phillips, professor of art, SUNY New Paltz, editor, Art Journal, College Art Association; Agata Olek Oleksiak, artist, with Ginger Wagg, dance artist; Michael Oatman, artist and assistant professor of architecture, Rensselaer Polytechnic Institute; Ian Berry, associate director, Frances Young Tang Teaching Museum and Art Gallery, Skidmore College and consulting director, Emerson Gallery, Hamilton College.

Participants: DeWitt Godfrey, Deborah Pokinski, Susanna White.

OCTOBER 7, 2006 – JANUARY 28, 2007

Substance and Light: Ten Sculptors with Cameras
Munson-Williams-Proctor Arts Institute, Utica NY

Garth Amundson, David Baskin, Isidro Blasco, Jiyoung Chae, Ipek Duben, Jane Edden, Liza McConnell, Steven Pippin, Sterz, Toni Vandergrift and Simon Lee's *Bus Obscura*
Sponsored by Munson-Williams-Proctor Arts Institute, Moon and Star project and the New York State Council on the Arts

OCTOBER 15 – DECEMBER 21, 2006

Light/Sound/Action: Art and Technology
Utica College, Utica NY

David Bowen, Daniel Bruce, Daniel Buckingham, Peter Forbes, Ianthe Jackson, David McQueen, Cristin Millett, Joel Murphy, Kaoru Sakurai, Allison Wiese
Sponsored by Special Metals Corporation and BGM Supply. Additional support from The Community Foundation of Herkimer & Oneida Counties, Inc. and Seifert Graphics Inc.

MAY 19 – OCTOBER 20, 2007

*Sculpture Space in Artland:
Art and Nature Intersecting*
Stone Quarry Hill Art Park, Cazenovia NY
Barbara Andrus, Emilie Brzezinski, Jonathan Kirk, John McCarty, Takashi Soga, John von Bergen
Panel discussion moderated by Daniel Buckingham
Sponsored by Stone Quarry Hill Art Park, with additional support from Sculpture Space

Related Exhibitions

FEBRUARY 1 – MARCH 2, 2007

Through a Fresh Lens: Images of Sculpture Space
Utica Public Library, Utica NY
T.R. Proctor High School Students document the creative process of 2006 residents of Sculpture Space. Rosalind Diamond, visual arts educator
Made possible with support from the Central New York Community Arts Council, Inc.; Arts in Education Institute

FEBRUARY 26 – APRIL 1, 2007

Atomic Baby: Recent Work by Carol Kinne
Colgate University, Hamilton NY

SUMMER 2006 – 2009

Ann Reichlin, *Translucent Home*
Sculpture Space, Utica NY
Work-in-progress

The 30th-anniversary projects are supported in part by The Community Foundation of Herkimer & Oneida Counties, Inc. and the Rosamond G. Childs Fund.

SculptureSpace

Sculpture Space is an international non-profit artist-in-residence program that has been in existence since 1976. The program has played an essential role in the establishment and advancement of the careers of upwards of 400 national and international artists. Dedicated to the concept that art, particularly sculpture, has the power to strengthen our understanding of the world around us, Sculpture Space strives to provide an environment conducive to fostering the creative process in its myriad manifestations.

The program provides emerging, mid-career and established artists with studio work-space, technical assistance, specialized equipment, financial support and time to engage fully in artistic exploration and to create sculpture on a scale that they otherwise might not be able to afford or accomplish outside such an environment.

Each year an Artist Review Panel, composed of arts professionals, artists and a distinguished guest, selects up to 20 artists from among *circa* 150 applications for the opportunity to partake in a two-month residency in Utica, NY, a former industrial city located on the Mohawk River in upstate New York.

Sculpture Space seeks as well to provide cultural enrichment to the Utica community and to expand public awareness of and support for contemporary art by creating opportunities for the resident artists to share their work with the public through work-in-progress exhibitions, lectures, tours, receptions and educational outreach.

[page 87]

EKKEHARD ALTENBURGER
KINO (CINEMA), 2005
Mixed media
Variable dimensions
Created during Sculpture Space residency
Installation at Sculpture Space
Photograph courtesy of the artist
Sculpture Space archives

[this page]

JONATHAN KIRK
Predator: or Better to Eat You With, 1994
Galvanized steel
4.3′ x 11′ x 3.8′
Installation at Hamilton College
Courtesy of Emerson Gallery, Hamilton College
Photograph by Richard Walker

[page 90]

CLAUDIA VIEIRA
WaterLINE: NYC–Utica, 2004
Magic marker, continuous line
c. 9 miles
Created during Sculpture Space residency
Courtesy of the artist
Photograph by Grady Gerbracht

Origin and Evolution/Forge and Scissors: A History of Sculpture Space

THOMAS E. PICHÉ, JR., pages 13–23

1   The sign, designed and fabricated by then-studio manager Takashi Soga with help from his son, Taiki Soga, is the result of a project led by then-board president Kim Lambert and supported by a grant from the Utica National Group Foundation, with additional assistance from O.W. Hubbell, Pacemaker Steel and contributions from past and current Sculpture Space board members.

2   Mike Powers, "Sculpture Space Enters a New Age," *Sculpture* (March/April 1988): 21.

3   For an expanded early history of Sculpture Space see Mary E. Murray, "A Score for Shaping Space: A Brief History," in *Sculpture Space: Celebrating 20 Years* (Utica, NY: Munson-Williams-Proctor Arts Institute, 1995), and Bruce Kaufmann, "Boiler Works Studio for Sculptors," *The Sunday Observer-Dispatch* (Utica, NY), February 29, 1976.

4   Carolyn Jabs, "Cooperative Studios: Sculpture Space, Utica, New York," *American Artist* (February 1981): 136.

5   Bernadine Lohden to John von Bergen, January 19, 2006. My thanks to John von Bergen for sharing this information with me.

6   John von Bergen, correspondence with the author, March 13, 2006.

7   Carolyn Jabs, 136.

8   Bruce Kaufmann, n.p.

9   *Ibid.*

10 From the beginning, Empire Recycling has been a major donor of materials to Sculpture Space. David Weitzman, a vice-president of the salvage yard, was the first board president of the residency program. In 2005 Steven Kowalsky, president of the company, and his brother Edward, the vice-president, began sponsoring an Earth Day arts project, donating materials to artists to create sculptures for the annual CHAIRity auction.

11 For more information on the "Bennington Group" see Charlotta Kotik, *The State of an Art: Sculpture Enters the 21st Century*, p. 26, in this volume.

12 Charlie Fisher, as quoted in Carolyn Jabs, 136.

13 Carolyn Jabs, 79; Morris Brown, "The World of Cold Steel Provides Crucible for Sculpture's Metal Men," unidentified clipping, box 14, Sculpture Space archives, Utica, NY.

14 Willard Boepple's 1977 *John Deere & the Lady's Claim*, exhibited from April 3–24, 1977, at the Munson-Williams-Proctor Institute of Art, was created during his residency at Sculpture Space; *Glencairn*, also a Sculpture Space product, appeared at Syracuse University's Joe & Emily Lowe Art Gallery in 1978. Boepple writes in 2006: "I made about thirty sculptures at Sculpture Space — most of them in the Steam Engine itself in the dead of winter and the next year in the Federal Building. It was such a terrific period both for me and for the up & coming Sculpture Space project. Von Bergen, Charlie, Bill Tucker, Lee [Tribe], [Del] Geist — the joint was jumping ... All these pieces are corten steel — from a mill order I made of 40,000 lbs which was dropped in the Federal yard one wintry day with an almighty whack."

15 Willard Boepple to David Weitzman, September 27, 1977; Del Geist to "Dear Friends," September 29, 1977; Clement Greenberg to Bernadine Lohden, September 28, 1976; box 12, Sculpture Space archives.

16 Lohden to von Bergen, January 19, 2006.

17 Rosette Schureman, a graduate in the first class at the newly accredited Munson-Williams-Proctor Arts Institute School of Art, was the first paid executive secretary at Sculpture Space, answering to Bernadette Lohden. Schureman's wages were paid in part by CETA, and when the funds ran out she suggested to Sylvia de Swaan, who was on the board at the time, that she become the director. Schureman says that for her Sculpture Space was "an intellectual gold-mine — like being in a Piranesi etching, like being in the middle of Pittsburgh in its heyday." James Iritani served as the first studio manager.

18 Sylvia de Swaan, telephone conversation with the author, March 6, 2006.

19 Sylvia de Swaan, "Sculpture Relating to Industry, *Sculptors International* 1, no. 3 (1982): 13; Jonathan Kirk, "Search for New Artists," April 3, 1981, open letter, box 2, Sculpture Space archives.

20 Press release, May 2, 1981, box 2, Sculpture Space archives.

21 Sylvia de Swaan, conversation with the author; Jonathan Kirk as quoted in Ellen Portnoy Abelove, "Boiler Works Artists," *Ford Times* (September 1982): 9.

22 During her first residency in 1992, Rosa Valado stayed with the film curator Scott MacDonald and his wife for three months; honorary board member Eleanor Levin recalls that she and her husband, the late Gerald Levin, housed an artist in the 1990s; and Charlie and Jan Fisher also remember artists staying with them over a period of years.

23 NYSCA funded seven New York State artists in 1996; six in 1998; and eight in 2001. In 2004, with encouragement from NYSCA, Sculpture Space began to provide its New York artists with free housing and transportation stipends. By 2005 the New York artists no longer received direct funding from the state for their stipends; rather, Sculpture Space, encouraged by an increased General Operating Support grant from NYSCA (which most recently was the largest of any artist workspace in the state) now provides the stipends from monies raised at special events.

24 Jan Pardee, who married Charlie Fisher, is a notable exception, attending Sculpture Space in 1976 and 1977.

25 Since 1976 Sculpture Space has welcomed artists from 23 countries.

26 According to Jonathan Kirk and Sylvia de Swaan the building purchase was one of the most important events in the organization's history. As Kirk recalls, "After the Fisher family sold the Utica Steam Engine and Boiler Works to the Heat Extraction Corporation there were discussions with the new landlords in an attempt to buy the studio building. A subdivision of the whole property, placing Sculpture Space on its own parcel of land, was approved, bringing the potential purchase one step closer to a reality. But when, in 1982, the USE & BW declared Chapter 11, lien holders besieged the Sculpture Space office. In the end, the city of Utica claimed everything for back taxes and made ready to sell all to the highest bidder. Determined to acquire the building as a permanent home for Sculpture Space, de Swaan mounted a letter-writing campaign to convince city officials of the uniqueness of the workshop and its value as a cultural asset to both the city of Utica and the state of New York. Kitty Carlisle Hart, chair of the New York State Council on the Arts, contacted the mayor's office and letters arrived from all over the state urging the city to do everything within its power to help. However, Mayor Lou La Polla insisted his hands were tied. 'By law,' he said, 'we have to accept the highest bid and that's just what we plan to do here.' De Swaan and Kirk talked to everyone they knew of who had been interested in purchasing the two-parcel property, trying to convince them to let Sculpture Space bid on its subdivided portion. Some agreed, but others had no interest in further discussion. December 12, 1985, the day of the public auction, finally arrived. By this time the city was totally supportive, but powerless to effect the outcome. De Swaan's opening bid was accompanied by an impassioned speech. The bidding that followed was brief. Words

#31 mentions GHAC

headline in the Utica *Observer-Dispatch* read *'Sold! Sculpture Space Saves Its Building.'"*

27 Sylvia de Swaan, conversation with the author.

28 The mission statement was clearly defined in 2004. Currently board president Kirk Pillow is leading an effort to update the by-laws.

29 This was to be the last Triennial Art Auction.

30 At the time Murtagh left Sculpture Space in 2002 a third of the $100,000 goal had been met.

31 The Greater Hartford Arts Council, under the directorship of Ken Kahn, an alumnus of Hamilton College and a former director of the Kirkland Art Center, was a strong client.

32 Sculpture Space received $15,000 from the Warhol Foundation to replace the equipment Jonathan Kirk took with him when he left the studio in 2000; the Trust for Mutual Understanding granted $36,000 to fund three artists at Sculpture Space from the Czech Republic, and three Sculpture Space artists at Cimelice Castle in the Czech Republic; the Community Foundation has awarded 16 grants through 2006 for in excess of $136,000.

33 Gina Murtagh, interview by author, Cazenovia, NY, March 8, 2006.

34 Although at the time of the celebrations she was no longer executive director of Sculpture Space, de Swaan had planned all three exhibitions prior to her departure. She was the keynote speaker for the autumn exhibition, *Sculpture Space: Celebrating 20 Years,* at the Munson-Williams-Proctor Arts Institute, and the show's organizer, Mary E. Murray, curator of contemporary art there since 1991, dedicated the catalogue to her. *Sculpture Space: 20th Anniversary, Drawings by Sculptors* ran from October 15–November 7, 1995 at the Kirkland Art Center, with works by Roberley Bell, Chris Duncan, Charles Fisher, Jeanne Flanagan, Lou Getty, Ronald Gonzalez, Christine Heller, Carol Kinne, Jonathan Kirk, John Knecht, Les LeVeque, Paul Mauren, James McDermid, Jim Morris, John von Bergen, Gail Scott White; and *Sylvia de Swaan: Work-in Progress/Twenty Years at Sculpture Space* appeared at SculptureCenter.

35 *INTER/CHANGE: Five Sculpture Space Artists at Stone Quarry Hill Art Park, Cazenovia, NY* was on view from June to October 1997 and exhibited works by Emilie Benes Brzezinski (*Charred Lintel* and *Reconstructed Arch*); Marek Ranis (*Le Vent des Forets,* from his ecological sculptures series); Yasafumi Takahashi (*Injurious Inertia* and *STRATA* – the tree); Monika Kulicka (*Reconstructions*); and Margie Neuhaus (*Memory Swim: Ascending*). Kulicka's work remained on view until the spring of 2006.

36 In the summer of 2006 Ann Reichlin began work on her site-specific piece, *Translucent Home,* to be installed on the 19th-century stone foundation. The project is supported by a NYSCA Decentralization grant administered by the Central New York Community Arts Council and awarded in collaboration with GroWest, a non-profit community development agency. See also in this volume Charlotta Kotik, *The State of an Art: Sculpture Enters the 21st Century,* p. 38.

37 *Urban Identity/Personal Architecture: Five Sculptors Revisit Utica, NY,* ran from June 5–August 28, 2000, and featured Karl Jensen's *Primitive Hut,* installed at 268 Genesee Street; Jerilea Zempel's *Caryatis Manouren,* at Old Tavern, Bagg's Square; Susan Meyer Fenton's *Escape, a love song for Harry and Bess,* at 100 Genesee Street; Isidro Blasco's *Three Projected Shadows,* at Union Station; and Joanna Przbyla's *Silence,* at Hanna Park. The show was supported by grants and in-kind support from the Rosamund G. Childs Fund and The Community Foundation of Herkimer & Oneida Counties, Fleet Bank, the City of Utica, the Kopernik Memorial Association, NYSCA, the Oneida County Convention and Visitors Bureau and Utica Monday Nite.

38 The Prospect Mountain exhibit in 1979 is a case in point. For more information on that exhibit see in this volume Charlotta Kotik, *The State of an Art: Sculpture Enters the 21st Century,* endnote no. 9, p. 93.

39 An example of this is the 11th International Sculpture Conference held in Washington, DC, in 1980. Coinciding with the fifth anniversary of Sculpture Space, the occasion brought attention to the organization and allowed it to highlight work made by eight of the 40 artists the workshop had accommodated to date, including William Tucker, John von Bergen, Richard Friedberg, Charles Fisher, Lee Tribe, Del Geist and James Iritani.

40 Sculpture Space artists who recently have worked in the community include Irish artist Caoimhghin O'Fraithile, whose *Longhouse* was created in Union Station; Allison Wiese, who displayed a provocative text on the marquis of the Stanley Theater; artists whose storefront installations were part of the Utica Monday Nite cultural program; and Jeff deCastro, who worked with local children from an afterschool group and put his bamboo *Space Ship* in the Children's Museum.

41 Waller is the founding director of Gallery 53 in Cooperstown, NY. She has served as director of development and public affairs at the New York State Historical Association, and as the executive director of the Lake Placid Institute for the Arts and Humanities and the New York State Alliance for Arts Education, an affiliate of the Kennedy Center.

42 Among the closed residency programs are the Johnson Atelier, Hamilton, NJ, and Capp Street Project in San Francisco.

43 Sydney Waller, interview by the author, Utica, NY, February 8, 2006; telephone conversation with the author, March 31, 2006; "From the Director," *Sculpture Space News* 2, no. 2 (October 2003): 3.

44 To maintain close ties to the resident artists, Waller has initiated a Thursday tea in the studio, during which time numerous issues are resolved.

45 The 30 anniversary series, *Sculpture Central International,* which consisted of two years of exhibitions, programs and events held during 2006 and 2007 in a variety of venues in Central New York, represents an important new direction for Sculpture Space. Works by a number of artists, all past residents of the program, were seen throughout the region, from as far away as Oneonta, Cazenovia, Hamilton and Clinton, bringing new interest in and appreciation of the program to an expanded Central New York audience. See p. 86 in this volume for a listing of the anniversary events and the Sculpture Space artists who participated.

46 In 2003 Northland Communications supported DSL service to Sculpture Space, the same year the program purchased its first camcorder; Wi-Fi was introduced in 2005 and two 3M video projectors and a Mac G5 computer for the artists, with up-to-date software, were bought in 2005 and 2006.

47 See Margaret Mathews-Berenson, *Urban Utopia: The Sculpture Space Promise,* endnote no. 3, p. 94 in this volume for more information on the Reichlin and Mustard houses.

The State of an Art: Sculpture Enters the 21st Century

CHARLOTTA KOTIK, pages 25–59

1 *The American Heritage® Dictionary of the English Language,* fourth edition. (Houghton Mifflin Company, 2004). <http://dictionary.reference.com/search?q=sculpture&x=0&y=0>.

2 Rosalind Krauss, Passages in Modern Sculpture, (New York: The Viking Press, 1977).

3 James Iritani (resident 1975, 1976, 1977, 1978, 1979),

who attended nearby Hamilton College, first became involved with Sculpture Space as John von Bergen's former student at the Munson-Williams-Proctor School of Art. (This was a recently accredited two-year degree program at the time). Iritani was the first hired studio manager of Sculpture Space.

4 Although not a formal name, the "Bennington Group" — or group — consisted of a number of artists, each of whom had some kind of relationship with either the town of Bennington, VT, or with Bennington College itself, in the 1970s and 1980s. Richard Friedberg recalls: "My memory is that it was a bit more complicated. Certainly among the earliest participants only Brower Hatcher and Jan Pardee (now Fisher) had direct ties to Bennington. Brower did, indeed, teach at Bennington College and Jan was a recent graduate. The only tie to Bennington that John von Bergen and I shared was that both our wives had gone to college there and had known each other. There were several early participants in the mid- and late 1970s who lived in the Bennington area and learned of the project through Brower and word of mouth. Isaac Witkin, Willard Boepple, Bill Tucker, Tim Scott and some others all had some connection to either Bennington and/or to Anthony Caro, who for a time was a visiting artist at Bennington College (Caro also taught at Syracuse University, a 50-minute drive from Sculpture Space). The term 'Bennington Group' became shorthand for a number of young sculptors who made sculpture out of steel in extended space, many of whom were influenced by Caro and his ilk."

John von Bergen adds: "If they were called 'The Bennington Group' it would have been a rather casual reference. ... There were, in truth, a large number of Bennington-associated artists, and dare I include Clement Greenberg as the champion of many of these artists, but 'The Bennington Group' ... wasn't used by me to refer to Bill Tucker, Willard Boepple, Brower Hatcher, Jan Pardee (Fisher), Marsha Pels, Isaac Witkin, Lee Tribe, James Wolfe."

Sylvia de Swaan, Sculpture Space executive director at the time, remembers "there were references to the Bennington School in the early years — artists with a certain gestalt and aesthetic point of view — mostly male, formalist, large, steel object makers — who dominated the roster in the early days of Sculpture Space."

5 Mary E. Murray, *Sculpture Space: Celebrating 20 Years,* (Utica, NY: Munson Williams Proctor Institute Museum of Art, 1995). Pp. 7, 9–18.

6 A rotating guest juror is invited to join the Artist Review Panel comprising up to seven alumni artists and arts professionals. The panel assesses the applications with the criteria of originality, quality and potential for growth, to select 20 artists. In the last four years the panel has reviewed between 130 and 180 applications each year from as many as 30 countries and 28 states. Past guest panelists have included art consultant Nancy Rosen, sculptor Mel Edwards, art critic Irving Sandler, artist Tom Nussbaum; Cee Scott Brown, executive director, Creative Time; Mary E. Murray, curator of contemporary art, Munson-Williams-Proctor Arts Institute; Carlos Gutierrez Solana, executive director, Artist Space; Dennis Elliott, Marie Walsh Sharpe Foundation.

7 This defining experience is described by Kenseth Armstead, a 1997 resident, in an email to the author on April 27, 2006: "The experience of working at Sculpture Space was a pivotal one for me. My work was in transition. I was shifting from being a primarily collaborative artist in the art-band X-Prz to my own (then-developing) unique artistic practice. Sculpture Space's facilities, equipment and full funding of my residency allowed me to immediately spread out, collect and then focus on creating outside New York City's many distractions and constant negotiations with space anemia. All I had to do was to make as much work as I could. I took full advantage. ... The work I completed there launched my career."

8 John von Bergen Sculpture Online: About the Artist. 2006. September 12, 2006 <http://www.johnvon bergen.com/artist.html>.

9 *The Prospect Mountain Sculpture Show: An Homage to David Smith,* ran from August 1–October 15, 1979, at Prospect Mountain, NY, near Lake George and Smith's Bolton Landing, NY, studio. The outdoor exhibit, organized by the Lake George Arts Project, Inc., included works by former Sculpture Space residents Charles Fisher, Richard Friedberg, Dan George, Brower Hatcher, Lee Tribe, William Tucker, John von Bergen and Isaac Witkin and was reviewed by John Ashbery in *New York Magazine,* August 27, 1979.

10 *Cai Guo-Qiang on the Roof: Transparent Monument,* The Metropolitan Museum of Art, April 25–October 29, 2006.

11 Greenberg's vital contribution to the early history of Sculpture Space is discussed in this volume by Thomas E. Piché, Jr. in *Origin and Evolution/Forge and Scissors: A History of Sculpture Space,* p. 16.

12 For further information see *Robert Rauschenberg: Combines,* The Metropolitan Museum of Art, December 20, 2005–April 2, 2006.

13 Walter de Maria created the *Mile-Long Drawing* in 1968 In the Mojave Desert, California; in Mormon Mesa, Nevada, Michael Heizer incised *Double*
Negative in 1969; in 1970 Robert Smithson built a jetty into the Great Salt Lake at Rozel Point, Utah; James Turrell still perfects the construction, begun in 1972, in Roden Crater, the dormant volcano in Painted Desert, in northern Arizona.

14 *Sculpture Space Inside/Outside* was on view at Hamilton College, Clinton, NY, from May–October 2006; the Outside component ran from May–October; Inside appeared at the college's Emerson Gallery from June 2–September 10.

15 Henry Frechette, "Sculpture Space in Utica brings art to Hamilton," *The Spectator,* Hamilton College (Issue 24. April 28, 2006). < http://spec.hamilton. edu/arts.cfm?action=display&news=1513>.

16 For another example of public memorials see Rand Carter, Utica, *The City Sculpture Space Calls Home,* p. 64 in this volume for Rainer Maria Wehner's *Homage to Wayne Newton Palmer* (2005), at Utica College.

17 D. Pokinski, *Sculpture Space Inside Outside* (Emerson Gallery, 2006).

18 Ann Reichlin, statement of the artist, January 2007.

19 Lynne Yamamoto used nails found at Doyle Hardware for a piece about her grandmother that appeared in *Sculpture Space: Celebrating 20 Years,* October 21 to December 31, 1995, at the Munson-Williams-Proctor Arts Institute and was subsequently shown at PS1 in New York City; Eddy Steinhauer also took advantage of the materials from Doyle.

20 Isidro Blasco, email to the author, May 14, 2006.

21 Rosa Valado, letter to the author, May 2, 2006.

22 *Meg Webster: Garden and Sculpture,* was on view at the Contemporary Arts Museum Houston November 1992–March 1994.

23 Architect Gregg Lynn coined the term "blob architecture" in 1995 to mean, according to Bell, "a new form of architecture which is fluid and free form. Seemingly organic in appearance, it only exists because of CAD and the ability of the computer to generate these liquid, fluid amoeba-shaped, blobby forms." Statement of the artist, January 13, 2007.

24 Roberley Bell, email to the author, May 4, 2006.

25 *Emilie Benes Brzezinski,* Galeria ZPAP, (Warsaw, Poland, 1992), p.7.

26 Statement of the artist, received January 2007. Regarding this work, Millett writes, "The architecture of an anatomy theater creates a power

relationship between the inhabitants of this space depending on their roles and locations in the theater. When in an anatomy theater, one has a heightened awareness of the inequality among the occupants, and one's role as 'viewer' or 'viewed' comes into question."

27   David Baskin, email to the author, May 11, 2006.

28   David Baskin, Black & White Gallery, Brooklyn, NY, statement of the artist, 2003.

29   Heavy-duty metal worktables, temporary walls and various pieces of bulky machinery, including table saws, presses, MIG and TIG welders, plasma cutters, welding tanks (OXY-Acetylene, Argon, CO2) and hoists, are stationed throughout the studio at Sculpture Space. For more information see Thomas E. Piché, Jr. *Origin and Evolution/Forge and Scissors: A History of Sculpture Space*, p. 13 in this volume.

30   The tree trunks used for these pieces were donated to the artist at Sculpture Space by the Utica Department of Public Works.

31   While at Sculpture Space, and as a result of visits to the studio from Mary Murray, curator of contemporary art at the Munson-Williams-Proctor Arts Institute, Yamamoto's *Resplendent* appeared at the institute from March 8–April 27, 2003.

32   Carrie Scanga, statement of the artist, January 2007.

33   Other Sculpture Space artists who address socio-political issues include Becky Shaw (2001–2002) Rainer Maria Wehner (1999–2000; 2002–2003), Mark L.F. Nicholson + Arad Shoham (2002–2003), Jenny Polak (1994), Annie West (1995–1996), Elizabeth Cohen + Michael Talley (1996–1997), Yasufumi Takahashi (1996–1997), Renee Ridgway (1995–1996).

34   Christy Rupp, statement of the artist, January 2007.

35   Kenseth Armstead, email to the author, April 27, 2006.

36   David Kramer, email to the author.

37   The use of a *camera obscura* goes back to the Arabic scientific discoveries of the tenth century. It is believed that Vermeer and other Dutch artists might have used the technique, but it is not known to what extent. Marcel Duchamp also used the *camera obscura* in his work, as did David Hockney.

38   Lee's *Bus Obscura* was on view in Utica October 7, 2006, at the Munson-Williams-Proctor Institute Museum of Art as part of the opening of the museum's show, *Substance and Light: Ten Sculptors*

Use Cameras, one of the celebrations of the 30th anniversary of Sculpture Space, and courtesy of the ArtsMix program of the Institute for the Creative and Performing Arts, Colgate University.

39   Mary E. Murray and Gina Murtagh, *Substance and Light,* p. 9.

Utica, The City Sculpture Space Calls Home
RAND CARTER, pages 62–65

1   The one-piece woolen undergarment known as the "Union Suit" was a local innovation, and many older Americans will remember the J. P. Stevens advertising campaign of the 1940s and '50s which featured a voluptuous, scantily-clad woman with the caption, "She lives in Boston, but she sleeps in Utica (sheets, that is)."

2   St. Agnes, 700 Kossuth Avenue; St. Mary's, 421 South Street; St. Mary of Mt. Carmel, 648 Jay Street; St. Louis Gonzaga, 520 Rutger Street; and St. Basil's, 901 Sherman Drive.

3   Union Station was built in 1914 by the New York architects Allen H. Stem and Alfred Fellheimer.

4   Mark Abilgaard was at Sculpture Space in 1985 and again in 1986; his work, *Passage* (1985) is on the campus of Utica College. James Iritani was a resident (and studio manager) in 1975, 1976, 1977, 1978, and 1979; *Trustan #5* (1979) is at the Munson-Williams-Proctor Arts Institute. James McDermid's *Historical Bell Monument,* made in collaboration with the Very Reverend Walter Madej, is dedicated to the Utica mill workers of the 19th and 20th centuries. McDermid was at Sculpture Space in 1976, 1977, and 1979. Wang Po Shu's five-part work, *Energy Sources* (1992) was begun during the Hong Kong-born artist's residency at Sculpture Space; Georgina Batty was at Sculpture Space in 2005, Rainer Maria Wehner was a resident in 1999–2000 and 2002–2003; his *Homage to Wayne Newton Palmer (2005)* is on the campus of Utica College. Jonathan Kirk was a resident (as well as studio manager) from 1980 through 1991, continuing as studio manager until 2000. His *Endowed Chair* is located near the *Eagle* in Roscoe Conkling Park. John von Bergen, a resident artist each year from 1975 to 1977, created *Bagg's Piece,* which was installed across Main Street from Union Station in 1981.

Urban Utopia: The Sculpture Space Promise
MARGARET MATHEWS-BERENSON, pages 67–77

1   The Ragdale Foundation, Lake Forest, IL; Djerassi Resident Artists Program, Woodside, CA; Ucross

Foundation Residency Program, Clearmont, WY; Yaddo, Saratoga Springs, NY; Millay Colony for the Arts, Austerlitz, NY; The MacDowell Colony, Peterborough, NH.

2   A second studio was added in December 2006 to accommodate the changing needs of the residents.

3   Until June 2006 two other distinctly different buildings also marked the site: The Reichlin House was an abandoned two-story, 100-year-old green clapboard house which served as a temporary site for Ann Reichlin's stainless steel sculpture *Insert,* of 1998, which slashed through the house leaving gaping holes; and the Mustard house, another late 19th-century structure, named for the family that once owned it. Following a fire in the Mustard house in June 2006, both were demolished in preparation for Sculpture Space's expansion initiative and campus development. Reichlin recently received a grant to create another sculpture to be built on the foundation of the original Reichlin House, taking the place of *Insert.* This new site-specific piece, *Translucent Home,* will consist of hundreds of rein-forcement rods, sheets of welded wire fabric and steel mesh, mimicking the form of the house, yet giving the appearance of a ghostly, dematerialized presence. A metaphor for fragility, transience and transformation, it seems a fitting homage to the evolution of Sculpture Space during its 30-year history, and a symbol as well of past, present and future. *Translucent Home* will be on view for several years as a 30th-anniversary exhibition project.

4   Bruce Kaufman, "Boiler Works Studio for Sculptors," *The Sunday Observer-Dispatch,* Utica, Sunday, February 29, 1976, n.p.; Mary E. Murray, *Sculpture Space: Celebrating 20 Years,* exh. cat., (Utica, New York: Munson-Williams-Proctor Institute Museum of Art, October 21 to December 31, 1995), pp. 9–11. For more information regarding the founding and purchase of Sculpture Space see Thomas E. Piché, Jr., *Origin and Evolution/Forge and Scissors: A History of Sculpture Space,* p. 13 in this volume.

5   In late 2006 Patrick Cuffe, a resident at Sculpture Space in 2004, succeeded Soga as studio manager.

6   Jonathan Kirk, interview with the author, February 20, 2006.

7   Sylvia de Swaan, interview with the author, April 23, 2006.

8   Wave Hill, Bronx, NY; Socrates Sculpture Park, Long Island City, NY; Snug Harbor Cultural Center, Staten Island, NY and DeCordova Sculpture Park, Lincoln, MA.

9   The residency program for 2007–2008 has been restricted to 11 months, leaving the month of December open.

10 The Bemis Center for Contemporary Arts, Omaha, Nebraska; Prairie Center of the Arts, Peoria, IL; McColl Center for Visual Art, Charlotte, NC; Isabella Stewart Gardner Museum, Boston, MA; The Mattress Factory, Pittsburgh, PA; Artpace, San Antonio, TX.

11 Today Sculpture Space offers each of its 20 artists per year a $2,000 stipend to help pay their residency expenses; housing is provided to all resident artists and bicycles are available to those without cars.

12 Franconia Sculpture Park, Shafer, MN; The Carving Studio and Sculpture Studio, West Rutland, VT; Roswell Artist-in-Residence Program, Roswell, NM; Evergreen House, Baltimore, MD; Montalvo, Saratoga, CA; Art in General, New York, NY; Smack Mellon, Brooklyn, NY.

13 John Michael Kohler Center, Sheboygan, WI; The Weir Farm Art Center, Wilton, CT; Vermont Studio Center, Johnson, VT.

14 Woodstock Byrdcliffe Guild, Woodstock, NY. Although Byrdcliffe did not establish an official residency program until 1988, it began as a self-sufficient artists' colony. Its founders embraced the aesthetics of the Arts and Crafts movement, welcoming artists, writers, playwrights, poets, composers and craftspeople to this rustic retreat in the Catskill Mountains. *Artists Communities: A Directory of Residencies That Offer Time and Space for Creativity*, ed. Deborah Obalil and Caitlin S. Glass (New York: Alworth Press, 2005), p. 82. Yaddo was founded in 1900; however, its residency program began in 1926. *ibid*, p. 222.

15 Black Mountain College Museum and Arts Center, Asheville, NC.

16 Penland School of Crafts, Penland, NC; Virginia Center for Creative Arts, Amherst, VA; Sculpture Space, Utica, NY;

17 Julia and David White Artists' Colony, Ciudad Colon, Costa Rica; Atlantic Center for the Arts, New Smyrna Beach, FL; Headlands, Sausalito, CA; Ucross; ArtCenter/South Florida, Miami Beach, FL.

18 Caitlin Strokosch, program and communications director, Alliance of Artists Communities, interview with the author, February 27, 2006.

19 Art Omi International Arts Center, Omi, NY.

20 Strokosch, *op. cit.*

21 www.artomi.org; About Art Omi, p.1.

22 Lynne Yamamoto, interview with the author, February 18, 2006.

23 Daniel Buckingham, interview with the author, February 20, 2006.

24 Steve Kowalsky, interview with the author, April 11, 2006.

25 John von Bergen, Charlie Fisher and Richard Friedberg, all practicing sculptors working in metal, provided the original impetus for the founding of Sculpture Space.

26 A list of art exhibitions, projects and events scheduled throughout central New York in 2006/2007 in honor of the 30th anniversary of Sculpture Space appears on p. 86; additional information is also in Thomas E. Piché, Jr., *Origin and Evolution/Forge and Scissors: A History of Sculpture Space*, endnote 38 in this volume.

27 From a statement by RoAnn M. Destito sent to the author via email on April 10, 2006.

Sculpture Central International 2006/2007
page 86

1 Sculpture Space organized a 30th-Anniversary Gala June 16, 2006. Over 300 guests feted the seven honorees who received the Sculpture Space Distinguished Service in the Arts Award: the three founding artists, Charlie Fisher, Richard Friedberg and Jon von Bergen; the original Sculpture Space staff, Sylvia de Swaan and Jonathan Kirk; and community arts leaders Joe Corasanti and Duff Matt. Arlene Somer chaired the 30th-anniversary steering committee. The committee included Vige Barrie, Joni Saylor Chizzonite, Lisa M. DeFrees, Susan W. Divine, Steve James, Pamela Jardieu, Virginia Kelly, Kim Lambert, Dale H. Lockwood, Sr., Catherine McEnroe, and Shirley S. Samuels. Fred and Carrie Matt served as co-chairs of the Honorary Gala Committee, and Ken Kahn, executive director, Greater Hartford Arts Council, served as Master of Ceremonies. The Honorary Committee included the Bank of Utica, Milton Bloch and Mary Karen Vellines, Dick and Kate Cardamone, Susan W. Divine, Robert W. Downes, Allen R. Freedman and Judy Brick Freedman, Dan George and Erica Marks, Nancy and Eric Huckaby, Kim Lambert, Dale H. Lockwood, Sr. and John Romanow, Mary Malone McCarthy and Michael Wade, McCraith Beverages, Inc., Mohawk Hospital Equipment, Inc., Albert Pylinski and Frank Ferrante, Mr. and Mrs. Alan Rosenblum, Frances Savett and Lester Wolfson, Paul D. Schweizer and R. Robert Sossen, Jr., Esq.

CHRIS DUNCAN
Water Table, 1981
White pine
26′ x 8′ x 4′
Courtesy of the artist
Sculpture Space archives

[end leaf]

KATARINA ISAKSSON
Photograph by Sylvia de Swaan, 1987